Memories of Hurricane Katrina and Other Musings

Jack O'Connor

Order this book online at www.trafford.com
or email orders@trafford.com

Most Trafford titles are also available at major online book retailers.

The picture on the opposite page is of Category 5 Hurricane Katrina in the Gulf of Mexico
heading for New Orleans and the Mississippi Gulf Coast. The photo was taken by a NASA
satellite on August 28, 2005 less than twenty-four hours before Katrina made landfall. The
picture is used courtesy of NASA, the National Aeronautics and Space Administration.

Printed in the United States of America.

ISBN: 978-1-4269-3727-9 (sc)
ISBN: 978-1-4269-3728-6 (hc)

Library of Congress Control Number: 2010910226

Trafford rev. 01/20/2011

 www.trafford.com

North America & international
toll-free: 1 888 232 4444 (USA & Canada)
phone: 250 383 6864 ♦ fax: 812 355 4082

This is a work which took nearly four years to write. I expect that some of my poems and stories will bring a tear to your eye and that others will put a smile on your face. More importantly, I trust that my words will allow you to see what I saw, hear what I heard, and feel what I felt during a great disaster. The television coverage of Hurricane Katrina showed the looting, shooting, burning and suffering. I hope you see, as I did, the goodness of man that this tragedy brought out. The television networks would not show you that.

This is not all about Katrina. It's about a change in me. It's about my life, which has been a pretty good ride..........so far! It's about people and events which have had an effect on me.

Jack O'Connor

Dedication

This work is dedicated to the victims of Hurricane Katrina. May God give comfort and strength to those who survived and may He take into His arms and grant eternal peace to those who did not. You will always be in my thoughts and prayers.

"I cried all the way [from Massachusetts] to South Carolina." Robin McGuffey, Dental Hygienist

"I suppose, and I think Jack would agree, that a poem, like the elephant to the blind man, is different to each beholder. Each person sees a different part of the whole enchilada. Having read the book, I speak for all those who – unless it's a Rudyard Kipling poem when you know for certain that a cigar is a cigar – have trouble figuring out the hidden meaning of a poem, or even if there was a hidden meaning, thanks for the back stories, Jack. Readers are doubly blessed by this book then, because not only are the poems labors of love, but the back stories are poetic, even as they explain what's what and who's who." Frank Emerson, Singer and Songwriter

"As I read this book, I was right there." Art Givens, Businessman.

"I enjoyed your book a lot. It gives people a good idea of the real meaning of a tragedy like Katrina and how it can impact a beautiful city and its people. I look forward to hearing that you have had it published." Michael Connelly, Author of "The Mortarmen".

Prologue

As a kid, I never really appreciated poetry because I couldn't understand how the teacher knew what the poet had in mind as he wrote his work. As I got older, I learned that they had answer sheets for the tests and they also had teacher editions of study guides. That must be how they knew what the poet was thinking when he wrote. Then I asked, "Who wrote the study guide?" I was pretty sure it wasn't the poet.

An acquaintance of mine, who graduated from American International College about twelve years before I did, tells an interesting story about an English Literature Professor. It seems my friend got in trouble in Prof. Duffy's class for arguing that Ernest Hemmingway's "Old Man and the Sea" was just a story about an old man who went fishing with no other meaning. Prof. Duffy insisted that it was full of symbolism. I understand they really got into it. I really enjoyed Prof. Duffy's classes. I just never understood how he was so smart that he saw meanings that I didn't even know were there. One day my friend went to a lecture by Ernest Hemmingway. Someone in the audience asked Hemmingway about the symbolism in "Old Man and the Sea" and he replied, "What symbolism? I just wrote a story about an old man who went fishing."

I don't know if the above story is completely accurate or not. It really doesn't matter. I think if someone pays attention to the words, he can get a pretty good idea of what the writer means, but you don't get the whole story. That's why so many intellectuals decide what the writer means and then pass it on to you.

My very good friend, Danny O'Flaherty wrote a song called "Coming Home, To You". If you listen to the words, you know that he is worried about what Hurricane Katrina will do to New Orleans. He tells of his emotions watching the devastation to the city. Danny and I talked about our feelings for New Orleans when we got together in April 2008 for the first time since July 2005. We talked about our desire to live there again, even though we probably never will, for different reasons. Danny's wife, Susan will not move back to Louisiana and I can't go through another hurricane. I know the anguish he felt watching the city he loved being destroyed, because he told me how it affected him. I had the same feelings. It is gut-wrenching to witness a city you love having its very soul ripped out. I had the same emotions as Danny and I tried to express them in "Home".

I think it is really fascinating to know why someone wrote a particular piece. I love to listen to interviews on the radio when an artist tells why he wrote a certain song. Even when a song seems to tell the whole story, there is usually something that triggered the idea for the song.

When I started writing poetry, I was not sure that I wanted someone trying to poke around in my head. Heck, I get lost when I try to roam around inside my own head! I didn't want to be responsible for someone getting lost in there and never being able to get out. What a horrible fate! Even I step outside of my head and go to "Fantasy Land" every now and again.

Since I didn't want anyone wandering around in my head, I decided to tell everyone why I wrote a poem. I wanted the reader to know what gave me the idea, what I was thinking, what I was feeling, what I was seeing, and what I was hearing. Having said all that, I realize that I failed. To give the whole story behind each poem would probably require writing an entire chapter for each poem. In "Katrina's Angels", I refer to people dying, "As generators in basements quit with a sputter." New Orleans has had flooding in the past. As a matter of fact, every time there are heavy rains, there is street flooding. Previous tropical storms have caused serious flooding without breaching the levees. Whenever this has happened, generators have been flooded and quit working. Generators and pumps tend to not work well under water.

A few years before Katrina struck the Gulf Coast, one of the storms that caused flooding in New Orleans also caused flooding in Houston. After that flooding, Houstonians decided to move computer equipment and generators, etc. to upper levels. The generator in the hotel where I was based was located on the roof (great idea). However, the fuel tank was nine floors below in the basement (not a great idea). Fortunately, our Director of Construction and the hotel maintenance man moved fifty-five gallon fuel drums to the roof to run the generator. Hospitals in New Orleans kept their generators in the basements. When these generators became flooded and quit, doctors and nurses had to ventilate patients by hand to keep them alive. Many did not survive.

However, I did try to give as much background as possible for every poem I wrote. I wanted the reader to see every scene as I did, whether that scene took place in New Orleans, in the skies over LaPorte, Texas doing aerobatics stunts or after a snow storm in New England.

If you insist on climbing inside my head, at your own risk, have at it! Read the poem first; analyze it, decide what I was thinking and what I meant. Then read the story and see how close you came. Otherwise, read the story first and as you read the poem, you will understand my message.

The bottom line is I hope this work will be informative and that you enjoy reading 'Memories of Hurricane Katrina and Other Musings". It has been a labor of love, filled with pain and joy.

Approx. 5:00PM on August 31, 2005, I loaded my two cats into my old, beat up car, with floodwaters sloshing around on the floorboards, and we drove out of hurricane ravaged New Orleans. I had my cats, my twelve year old car with over two hundred thousand miles on it and the clothes on my back. I felt like a wealthy man. I was soon to learn just how rich I was.

I had been working as Director of Security for a hotel chain in New Orleans when Hurricane Katrina struck the city. Over the next three days, I was amazed that people who did not know if they would ever leave the hotel alive were concerned about me because I had to climb the stairs in an eight story hotel to check on their well-being and to bring them what little news we had received. There was no power in the city. The basement and the first floor were flooded and the water was coated with fuel oil. We finally evacuated the guests by late Wednesday afternoon and were able to leave the hotel ourselves.

Around 3:00AM on Thursday morning I was driving west on I-10 somewhere in Texas when I remembered that the previous year I had stayed in LaPorte, Texas when I had evacuated for Hurricane Ivan. I stopped at a Waffle House to use the pay phone. My tee shirt and shorts were oil stained and my sneakers were oil soaked and squished when I walked. My condition and the fact that I was going west led the waitress to conclude that I was coming from Louisiana. I asked her for change for a dollar so I could use the pay phone and without a second's pause, she said, "Here use my cell phone."

Later that morning, at a motel in Houston, I met a wonderful, elderly, black couple from New Orleans. When they told me where they lived, I knew that in that section of the city, houses were completely under water. They had lost everything and that wonderful woman looked at me and said, "I think you need a hug." They had left before Katrina struck. Her husband told me how to get to a church that was feeding lunch and supper to people from New Orleans.

My brother-in-law and his wife, who live in Houston, took me in. Linda was sick, but when she heard I was in town, she made arrangements for me to see a doctor for treatment of chemical burns. Jim, who among

1

other things is an aerobatics pilot instructor, was at an air show that weekend. He came home and took me to the show so that Linda could recuperate. While at the show, little six-year old Garrett came up to me and said, "I'm sorry you were in a hurricane, but I'm glad you got out."

Because of these angels of mercy, I decided to write a poem to say thank you to all of them. I wanted to have it made into a song. A very good friend of mine, singer and songwriter, Danny O'Flaherty, who lost both his home and pub due to Katrina, has agreed to write music for 'Katrina's Angels".

Katrina's Angels

Katrina came in roaring like a banshee.
Wind and rain raging in from the sea
After the storm, floodwaters sneaked
In killing young and old as it rose silently.

Amongst the devastation and horror,
Looting and shooting, fires and death,
People from around the world watched
Television reports and held their breath.

In their homes and shelters good citizens died,
Patients in modern hospitals fared no better
As generators in basements quit with a sputter
While the deadly floodwaters continued to rise.

Fear and despair seemed to rule the day
When Katrina's Angles appeared in this mess,
Common people filled with love and kindness
Helping friends and strangers in every way
Giving all they could; food, clothing and shelter
To help brothers and sisters survive the disaster.

Leaving this once great, now shattered city,
My mind in shock, my body was burned.
As we started our trek, I soon learned
People were giving their love, but not pity.

Fear and despair seemed to rule the day
When Katrina's Angels appeared in this mess,
Common people filled with love and kindness
Helping friends and strangers in every way
Giving all they could; food, clothing and shelter
To help brothers and sisters survive the disaster.

We went to the west and then back to the north,
Along the way seeing the trait that did the most
To make this great country the best on the earth
I know Americans will rebuild the Gulf Coast.

Fear and despair seemed to rule the day
When Katrina's Angels appeared in this mess,
Common people filled with love and kindness
Helping friends and strangers in every way
Giving all they could, food, clothing and shelter
To help brothers and sisters survive the disaster.

The Gulf Coast and a mighty city lay in rubble,
With promises to rebuild them greater than before,
Faced with so many problems, so much trouble,
With the help of God, we can accomplish the chore.

Fear and despair seemed to rule the day
When Katrina's Angels appeared in this mess,
Common people filled with love and kindness
Helping friends and strangers in every way
Giving all they could; food, clothing and shelter
To help brothers and sisters survive the disaster.

When the lights went out during Hurricane Katrina the Central Business District, which is usually bustling day and night became very dark and quiet. Monday night – Tuesday morning the 17th Street Canal levee was breached and the CBD was flooded. Around 10:00PM Tuesday, a large wave struck the front doors of the hotel sending even more water pouring into the lobby. A huge front end loader pulled up in front of the closed hotel across the street and the police officers who were staying there began loading their luggage into the bucket. One of the officers saw me standing in the doorway and yelled to me. He said, "Get up high. The water is supposed to rise."

At that time, I was the only manager in the hotel and I wondered if the others would be able to get back. Would I have to evacuate the guests by myself? Would we ever be able to get out of the hotel? I had plenty of time to think and I decided that I needed to make some major changes.

About two weeks before Katrina hit, I had a serious talk with one of our night auditors, who also happened to be an ordained Southern Baptist Minister and a friend. He suggested that if I read John in the Bible, I might find the answers I was seeking. We had emergency lighting in the corridors, at least while the fuel lasted, so I went to one of the rooms and got a Bible. I don't remember what John said, but I do know that I used the time to make peace with my Maker. I also had a serious discussion with God. For once I did not try to play "Let's Make A Deal". I did not ask God to let me survive, what I did ask for was the courage to face whatever was in store for me with dignity. I also asked that whether I had only minutes or years left to live, that He help me to change and live the way God wants us to live.

A great calm came over me and that was when my eyes opened and I began to see. When I graduated from American International College, I knew its motto, "Post Tenebras Lux" translated to "After Darkness Light", but I didn't really know its meaning until Katrina knocked out the lights in New Orleans.

Near the end of November 2006, I learned that Rev. Eric Patrick and his family survived Katrina. I talked with him on the phone and we prayed together. I told him about my experience in the hotel and how grateful I was to him for pointing me in the right direction. "Post Tenebras Lux" is dedicated to Eric for his helping me find the light.

Post Tenebras Lux

When I was born I had sight but I didn't see
The beauty that God had placed all around me.
When I was born I had ears but I didn't hear
Birds singing while flitting through the trees.

Katrina brought total darkness and silence
To a normally hustling and bustling city.
And that's when, for the first time in my life,
I began to see and hear the beauty that surrounds me.

I took for granted so many things for so many years
That it took total darkness for me to see the light.
I don't need to look hard now to see God's beauty.
I find it all around me when I use my gift of sight.

The beauty and joy in the simple things, a baby animal,
Laughter, children at Christmas, family, friends,
A river, the ocean, a sunrise or sunset, nature in general,
Fresh snow in the valleys and mountains, it just never ends.

The shape of a cloud, the stars in the sky, reflections on water,
Moon shining on snow, melodious sounds of music and rain,
The parent's devotion and love for a new son or daughter,
All make me desire to experience them again and again.

Good things come from bad and Katrina was the worst,
But it took the lights going out to give me my sight,
In the darkness my ears opened, but my eyes opened first,
Giving meaning to Post Tenebras Lux, After Darkness Light.

I have always believed that if a man had one or two friends he was a lucky man. Many old clichés are based on truth, such as, "A friend in need is a friend indeed." I never thought much about that cliché until after Hurricane Katrina.

Twenty-plus years working as a police officer left me rather cynical. I had seen the worst in people. In New Orleans, the looting, shooting and burning seemed to confirm my cynicism. Then I saw another side of common people; people doing little and large things to help complete strangers in time of need. People in Texas opened their hearts and wallets to help their neighbors from Louisiana. Businesses using their time and resources to collect food, and clothing, giving discounts to hurricane victims; even people pulling their houses off the market to help a stranger who had lost everything. There were also the small personal acts of kindness which meant so much to me.

From donating money, to personally giving a helping hand to a complete stranger, people were saying, "Let me help you my brother (sister), for I am your friend." I will never see many of these friends again, but I will never forget them. On behalf of other Katrina survivors I say, "God love you and I thank you all. You will always be my friend."

Friends

I know a lot of people but only have a few friends.
Acquaintances want to be around you when times are good.
Friends don't care about good times, but wish to stand
Beside you when it seems that your world is at an end.

If a man has a good friend, he is a lucky man indeed.
To have more than a handful of friends is very rare.
It only takes one good friend in time of need
To pick up the load and ease the burden you bear.

Hurricane Katrina brought misery and pain
To thousands whose world came to an end.
First came the wind, then the floods and rain,
That August day is relived over and over again.

What I said before is no longer true for me.
While reeling from shock, unable to comprehend.
A stranger would say either by word or deed,
"Let me help you my brother, for I am your friend."

Little things give comfort and make the heart swell.
A hug, the use of a cell phone, and much more tend
To make me fondly wish every one of you well.
Though I'll never see you again, I call you my friend.

So many people helped during my time of need.
In a disaster, human love doesn't know any end.
As I sit here and count I'm surprised to see
The number of people I can call my friends.

"Nature" came to me very quickly. All my other poems were written on a computer. "Karina's Angels" took several months and several revisions to write. The other poems underwent many revisions and rewrites.

One Saturday afternoon, I was going in to a diner to grab some lunch. I brought a notebook (not a laptop computer, but a paper notebook) into the diner with me. I had an idea for a poem about some of the natural disasters which had occurred over the past couple of years. The words flowed and by the time I had finished my burger, "Nature" was completed. What you see on the next page is exactly what I wrote in the notebook during lunch.

Every writer would give his eyeteeth to write something that needs no revisions. I am very fortunate to have it happen for this poem. If it never happens again, I still consider myself lucky that it occurred once.

I feel "Nature" contains a powerful message. I hope you enjoy it, but I hope, even more, that you heed its message and pay attention to our environment.

Nature

Nature came first and did very well.
Animals arrived and they lived in harmony.
Then man came and said, "This looks okay, but hell,
I just want to make a few improvements."

Left on its own, Nature works in balance,
Removing the weak, so the strong can survive.
In this way Nature gives all healthy species a chance
To exist and flourish as together they thrive.

Nature works in cycles to accomplish her chore.
Rain and drought, rich harvest and famine,
She uses all means to return to balance once more.
Through the eons this happened again and again.

Man in his 'wisdom' has sought to control all things.
Animals, his fellow man, the environment it didn't matter.
As long as he was in control, the world was his own.
That Nature might not agree was never a factor.

Man built levees, dammed rivers and streams,
Erected great cities below the level of the sea,
Built houses and towns in areas that flood,
And failed to get Nature's message, "That's not good!"

Man scarred the earth and stripped the forest
Stealing Nature's wealth without ever a pause,
Congress finally passed some bills, but was it too late
To pacify Nature with some environmental laws?

The Christmas 2004 Tsunami killed hundreds of
Thousands of humans, but very few animals shared their fate.
Did Nature warn the animals who respected Her,
And ignore man who did not? Wake up man before it's too late!

When I moved back north after living in New Orleans for seven years, I experienced my first winter in a long time. The first snow storm covered the ground with a blanket of white. I went out to shovel the driveway of the house where I was staying. I had always hated shoveling snow. The driveway was very large as there was a three car garage. To my amazement, I enjoyed being out in the cold and snow.

I found I enjoyed the beauty of the fresh fallen snow on the landscape. This prompted me to write the poem "Snow".

Snow

Gently it floats down from the sky
To cover the ground like a blanket,
So cold and clean, so pure and white,
So fluffy when dry, so heavy when wet.

As a child I loved the snow, making snowmen,
And angels in the snow, building snow forts,
Sliding down great hills, our noses felt frozen,
Snowball fights, good times, lots of fun of all sorts.

Adulthood arrived and snow was no longer any fun.
Shoveling walks and drives caused much back pain.
Sore muscles expected when shoveling was done,
Aspirin and liniment were used again and again.

A great disaster caused a huge change in me.
It opened my eyes, altered my thinking and so
I really appreciate being surrounded by beauty
And once again I can marvel at, and enjoy the snow.

The dazzling glare in the bright sunlight
And the soft glow from the moon at night
Nature's winter beauty is close at hand
As we travel through a Winter Wonderland.

The drifts and valleys caused by blowing wind,
Little whirlwinds of snow dancing to and fro,
Mountains' rocks and trees covered with snow,
New England winters bring these things to mind.

Gently it floats down from the sky
Drifting and howling as the winds blow,
Unleashing this special winter beauty
As once again I realize, I love the snow.

A few weeks ago (summer 2006) I met a wonderful woman while I was working. When I first saw her, I noticed that she was wearing a headscarf. My first thought was that she had cancer. But, how could that be? She looked so healthy and she was laughing and smiling. We started talking and she told me that she had just finished chemotherapy and was beginning radiation therapy. She said she was devastated when she was first diagnosed. She said that she decided the cancer might kill her, but it would never beat her. She feels that she can make others feel better with her positive outlook.

My brief encounter with that amazing woman has enriched my life. I wrote the following poem after meeting her. Special Lady, I don't know your name, but "Why Not Me?" is dedicated to you. Thank you.

Why Not Me?

I used to look at people who had riches and money
With jealousy and say, "Why them? Why not me?"
I disliked them without even knowing their name.
"It's not fair, it's really unjust." I would complain.

I saw a woman wearing a headscarf over her hair.
I thought she had cancer, but she was so happy,
So vibrant, she was living every moment with a flair.
Could she possibly be coping with the "Big C"?

She told me she had just completed chemotherapy
And was starting radiation therapy. What a pleasure
To talk with that wonderful woman. She is really
An inspiration to all she meets. Her attitude; a real treasure.

When she learned of her disease, she was discouraged.
But decided that while the cancer might kill her body,
She would fight it and by doing so became encouraged.
She said, "It may kill me, but I won't ever let it beat me."

Hurricane Katrina opened my eyes and is responsible for me
Making changes in how I now act and look at life.
People want to help, and be around those without strife.
A much happier and more pleasant man is the new me.

I thank that wonderful woman for brightening my day.
She reminded me of how much happier I am today.
For I can look at those less fortunate than me and say,
"Why them, Lord? Why not me? Thank you, God."

One evening during the winter of 2006, I talked with Delilah on the radio about it taking the lights going out in New Orleans during Hurricane Katrina for me to begin to see. For those who don't know who she is, Delilah has a nationally syndicated radio show on the air every evening. She specializes in love songs and dedications from listeners. She is very nurturing to her listeners who call in. A short time after our conversation, a woman who had been like a mother to Delilah passed away. Her name was Mary and I wrote a poem as a tribute to her.

Mary

Delilah, while I never got to meet your Mary
And would not have recognized her face,
I know that God has placed many 'Marys'
On earth to make His world a better place.

You spoke of Mary with so much love
Many of your listeners prayed for her.
We asked God to restore her health, but
He decided to bring her home to heaven above.

Mary not only touched upon your spirit
She also touched the spirits of your fans.
When you told of her love and kindness
We all felt the gentle touch of her hands.

Now you mourn your loss, but in your heart
You know that Mary is with God in heaven,
Receiving her reward for doing her part
To make this world a better place to live in.

We share your grief and pain, yet it seems to me
That when someone as good as Mary passes on
It is appropriate to celebrate the part of her journey
That brings her to our Lord in heaven for all eternity.

Thank God for the 'Marys' He has given this world
Their names may be different, but their plan is the same,
To enrich the lives of others, that is their goal.
God bless them for all they do in His holy name.

Most of the poems I have written to this point were rather serious and influenced by Hurricane Katrina and its effect on me. As I was writing this poem, I realized just how heavy it was turning out to be. I was nearly done with it when I decided to just screw around and have some fun.

Less than three weeks after Hurricane Katrina, I was having supper with my brother-in-law and his wife. Jim is both a glider pilot instructor and an aerobatics pilot instructor. I was planning on traveling from Houston to Massachusetts, where I was born and raised the following Monday. Jim said he wanted to take me flying before I left Texas. He asked if I wanted to go glider or aerobatics flying. Without a second's hesitation I replied that I always had more guts than brains, and would prefer aerobatics flying. Besides, there is no way anyone was going to get me to fly in a plane with no engine. That made about as much sense to me as jumping out of a perfectly good airplane........none!

I had never been so scared than when I was sitting in the flooded hotel, and not knowing if I would survive the aftermath of Katrina. Here I was less than three weeks later flying in an airplane doing stunts. The finale of the afternoon was climbing to 3500 feet and having the pilot stall the engine and push the stick forward and to the left. The result was pointing straight down while spinning counterclockwise with the engine shut off. It scared the hell out of me, but what a thrill. Thanks, Jim!

Have You Ever

Have you ever
    Broken up a barroom brawl?
    Been involved in a high speed chase?
    Quelled a riot on the mall?
    Gone into a building that was ablaze?
Well, I have.

Have you ever
    Faced an armed suspect on your own?
    Taken a body from a wrecked car?
    Pulled a raid in a drug dealer's home?
    Wrestled a drunk out of a bar?
Well, I have.

Have you ever
    Been spit on and called names for doing your job?
    Had someone hit you with a branch, a fist or a car?
    Had to stand up to an angry, unruly crowd?
    Told a parent the light went out in their child's star?
Well, I have.

Have you ever
    Gone through a major hurricane?
    And the aftermath, the flood and pain?
    Survived the fear of that, and I'm not lyin'
    Two weeks later, gone aerobatics flying?
Well, I did!

I have had an interesting life, so far. I used to say that I wish some things hadn't happened to me. I would ask, "Why me?" At times I would get angry with God for giving me so much crap. Katrina was devastating. I don't think anyone would fault me for saying that I wish it hadn't happened to me. Katrina changed me and I no longer wish something bad didn't happen to me. I am glad that I experienced Katrina. If I hadn't, I never would have changed my life, nor would I have ever met so many wonderful people, such as Katrina's Angels, or the wonderful people at CareerPoint, a one-stop career center in Holyoke, MA.

As a cop, I have seen and done some very unpleasant things. As tragic as some of the things people do to their fellow human beings are, and the effect they had on me, there were also some very positive events. It's a great feeling to arrest someone who has just committed a brutal rape, or who has just maimed a complete stranger just because of the color of his skin.

"Have You Ever II" is what I had in mind before I decided to fool around with the previous poem. I think it kind of explains who I am and how I came to be me.

Have You Ever II

Have you ever
    Broken up a barroom brawl?
    Been involved in a high speed chase?
    Quelled a riot on the mall?
    Gone into a building that was ablaze?
Well, I have.

Have you ever
    Faced an armed suspect on your own?
    Taken a body from a wrecked car?
    Pulled a raid in a drug dealer's home?
    Wrestled a drunk out of the bar?
Well, I have.

Have you ever
    Been spit on and called names for doing your job?
    Had someone hit you with a branch, a fist or a car?
    Had to stand up to an angry, unruly crowd?
    Told a parent the light went out in their child's star?
Well, I have.

These are the experiences that make up my life.
Some are sad while others are funny.
Many brought joy and others caused strife.
I wouldn't trade them for they are what make me; ME.

Every day you should thank our Father in heaven
For the soldiers, firefighters and police officers
Who do the tasks listed above without question
They risk it all; put their lives on the line for others.

They don't ask for headlines for their brave acts.
These heroic man and women ask you please
Pray to almighty God when they finish their tasks
At the end of the day, they return to their families.

When I arrived in Massachusetts in September of 2005, the words homeless, refugee and displaced person all applied to me. While I did not live under a bridge, thanks to the generosity of a friend who let me stay in his house, I was homeless. My apartment was located in Jefferson Parish LA, which was closed. I had fled from a place of danger to one of safety. I had definitely been displaced by Hurricane Katrina.

During the fall, winter and spring, I tried my best to be as unobtrusive as possible. My host arose around 4:00AM every day, so he went to bed early. He would have his lady friend over every evening and they would have supper together and spend the early evening together. I was always invited to eat with them, but I wanted them to have their time alone. I would spend my days looking for work, usually at CareerPoint in Holyoke, MA. I would then get some supper and I would go to my room. By the time I fed, and then spent some time with my cats, Denise had gone home and Merrill had gone to bed. While I was free to use the television, I usually didn't so I would not disturb Merrill. That gave me plenty of time to read and think.

Through a friend at CareerPoint, I bought a used laptop. I took my new treasure to my room and during the winter months, I wrote several poems. Many of them are directly related to Hurricane Katrina and its effect on me, some others are the result of the change in me brought on by Katrina.

The next five poems, "A Police Officer's Prayer", "Size Matters....Not", "Adam's Dream", "Our Friend" and "A Man I Admire" all came about because of my thoughts about Katrina and how it changed me, during the winter of 2005 – 2006. Judge Roy Moore was from Alabama, one of the states nailed by Katrina. While thinking of how I had changed because of Katrina, I thought of my friend Danny O'Flaherty. From there, the fifth anniversary of our friend, Butch Moore's death brought about 'Our Friend". "A Man I Admire" is about Danny so it was logical that it would come at that time. Since I was writing tributes, I included "Adam's Dream". It had nothing to do directly with Katrina, but because the 'new me' was now writing, and I had wanted to do something for Adam since his death, I wrote it.

There was a small end table next to the bed in my room. I had my laptop on top of that table. I was sitting on the side of my bed one evening with one foot resting on the shelf of the table and the other on top of one of the cat carriers. I had been thinking about Katrina and all the destruction and pain it had caused. I needed to relieve the stress. I thought of my mother and her sense of humor and got the idea for "Size Matters….Not". It was just an attempt to play around and have a little fun.

A southern judge, Judge Roy Moore lost his job because he would not remove the Ten Commandments from his courthouse. There is a move by a minority of people to rewrite the "Pledge of Allegiance" because it contains the words "under God". A man, who didn't even have custody of his daughter, filed suit in California and a federal court ruled that the "Pledge of Allegiance" could not be recited in public schools because it is a 'prayer'. In 1969, comedian Red Skelton closed a show with a piece on the "Pledge of Allegiance". As a child, his school principal explained the meaning of the "Pledge" word by word. Red concluded by saying that since his childhood two words, "under God" were added. He said, "Wouldn't it be a shame if someday someone decided it was a prayer and could not be recited in schools?" How prophetic for a man who never went to the eighth grade in school!

God is not allowed in public schools, but condoms are. God is not allowed in public buildings or at public meetings. They say there are no atheists in a foxhole. I also believe that there are no atheists in a squad car. The best description I ever heard of police work was told to me by a field training officer when I was a rookie. He said, "Police work is hours of tedious boredom interrupted by seconds of sheer terror." These thoughts led to my writing "A Police Officer's Prayer".

A Police Officer's Prayer

Dear God, I know you're not allowed in the schools,
The courts, or where government bodies meet,
But you are always welcome to ride in my cruiser,
And please, remain beside me as I walk my beat.

Please stay with me as I respond to a bank alarm,
A shooting, an accident or a fight in a bar,
A stabbing, domestic violence or a gang war,
There's no such thing as an atheist in a patrol car.

Throughout my tour of duty, I'll appreciate your
Company and guidance, your wisdom and sage,
Let my gun hand be quick enough to save one's life,
But also slow enough to avoid a terrible mistake.

Give me the compassion to comfort the victim,
Or the strength to console the next of kin,
Or the courage to confront the criminal
And lock him up to make it safe for all.

And please God, when my tour is at an end,
Let me leave the suffering and pain behind
So that I can return to my home and family
And attempt to live a normal life again. Amen.

My mother was a very short person, physically, but she was a giant in all other respects. She had a heart as big as all outdoors and a great sense of humor. However, if you were smart, you didn't want to get her Irish up, or she was liable to lower the boom on you. I was thinking about her a few months ago (winter 2006) when I got the idea to write "Size Matters.... Not".

While writing the poem, I thought of another friend of mine who is not as tall as my mother was. She too, has a big heart, and is very loving and generous. I don't think I would want to cross her either. I hope you enjoy this little tribute to two dear ladies mixed with a little bit of nonsense.

Size Matters....Not!

Tall is short, and short is tall!
Small is large, and large is small!
This may sound confusing to y'all
But it's not! Oh no! Not at all!

The atomic bomb was small,
But it made one hell of a big bang.
Big Ford Motor Company's Edsel
Made only a small whimper. Dang!

My mother stood less than five feet.
Her voice was soft and kind.
When she spoke you knew to heed
Her words or get a piece of her mind.

She raised two sons, one a real hellion.
And when she thought her work was done,
She decided to raise two granddaughters
And believe it or not, it kept her young.

I have a friend who's not as tall as mom.
She has a loving heart as large as can be,
Intelligent and gentle and oh sooo sweet,
Harm her and find you've set off a big bomb.

What is my point, you may ask?
With written words, have I said a lot?
Listen and see what I say. Your task
Is to decide if size matters or not.

Back in the early nineties, my mother-in-law, Edith Smolen befriended a NASCAR official and we were able to get into the pits and garages at the Winston Cup races in Dover, DE and Loudon, NH. As a result I got to meet all the drivers and many of the pit crewmembers. Edith is a big Richard Petty fan. I loved seeing how Richard and Kyle Petty would both take the time to give her a hug and talk with her every time she went to the track. They are both special people.

When Kyle's son, Adam was fifteen, I saw him racing Legend cars on television. One of the announcers mentioned that at age fifteen, Adam was a gentleman, just as his father and grandfather were. When I saw Kyle following spring, I told him about that and he beamed as any father would.

Adam was killed in practice in Loudon, NH in May 2000. It took six years to write "Adam's Dream" but it is for Kyle and Richard. Adam touched a lot of lives.

Adam's Dream

Adam Petty had a dream. He wanted to race
Just like his great-grandfather, grandfather,
And his father before him. He had the grace
And the talent, I think, to be as good as The King.

Adam was a real credit to the fine name of Petty.
By the age of fifteen, he was known as a gentleman.
He worked hard and studied and soon all could see
He would reach his goal while still a young man.

God's plan is not always the same as our own.
A brilliant career came to a halt that awful day
When Our Lord called Adam to his heavenly home.
When we don't know the reason, it helps if we pray.

Surely when Adam arrived at the heavenly gates,
Great-Grandpa Lee was there to take his hand
And introduce him to the legendary racing greats
Who immediately welcomed him to their band!

Now on heaven's great racetrack and in the celestial
Garage, as the famous drivers of old adjust their cars
Adam socializes with them and works by their side
And joins these great drivers as they race among the stars!

Adam Petty had a dream. If only he could pass the test
The world's best drivers would admit him to their crew.
In heaven's garage, he mingles with the best of the best.
I am convinced that Adam's dream really came true.

Adam Petty's photo on the previous page used by permission.
From the collection of Edith Smolen.

Edith Smolen and Richard Petty.
From the collection of Edith Smolen.

Left to right
Maeve Mulvaney Moore, the author,
Joanne O'Connor and Butch Moore.
From author's collection.

Butch & Maeve Moore
"Ireland's Dynamic Duo"
Photo from author's collection.

Butch Moore was the first singer to represent Ireland in the Eurovision Music Festival in 1965. He finished in sixth place singing "Walking the Streets in the Rain". I got to know Butch and his wife, Maeve Mulvaney Moore in the mid-eighties and we became good friends. Through Butch, I met Danny O'Flaherty, and when I moved to New Orleans, Danny and I became very good friends. Danny is a singer-songwriter from Connemara and until Katrina owned a marvelous pub in the French Quarter.

Unfortunately, Butch passed away in April 2001. On the fifth anniversary of his death, I wrote "Our Friend" for Danny. I also wrote it as a tribute to our good friend, Butch Moore.

Our Friend

On April 3, 2001, five years past
Danny O'Flaherty and I lost a good friend.
A great singer was taken so very fast,
Butch Moore, a native son of Old Erin.

The first to represent his native Ireland
Singing in the Eurovision music contest,
"Walking the Streets in the Rain"
Placed Butch Moore among Europe's best.

His rich clear voice ringing in our ears
Brought hours of pleasure to his many fans.
On stage he thrived on applause and cheers,
We were rewarded with more songs from the man.

He might forget lyrics, but never a name.
Ever quick with a smile, a laugh or a joke,
You always felt welcome where e'er he played
And loved his silly grin when he misspoke.

Nervous and timid, he returned to his home,
Many years later to do some concerts for fans
Who remembered, and again made him their own.
Which brought enormous pleasure to this humble man.

"They remembered me!", Butch stated so proud
When he returned home from his first Erin tour.
Several more followed with much larger crowds.
Butch was thrilled again to be the man of the hour.

His voice has been silenced, no more will he sing.
His fans will remember his songs and his legend.
For those lucky enough to know him, one thing
Is certain, we still love and miss our good friend......

Butch Moore.

Photo of Butch Moore on previous page used by permission.
Courtesy of Ian Gallagher.

Before I visited New Orleans for the first time, Butch Moore told me to look up a friend of his, Danny O'Flaherty. It took a couple of visits to the city, but I finally got to meet Danny. Danny is from Ireland and is a singer and songwriter. He has a passion for folk music and Celtic heritage. When I first met Danny, we hit it off immediately. We are both pretty closed-mouthed and don't talk about our inner feelings very easily, but we both opened up right away.

Danny does a lot of work with school children and performs many benefit concerts. He also does a great deal of work with the Special Olympics. In addition, he is involved in many programs to teach our heritage to children and adults, such as Celtic festivals, lessons in Irish language, dancing, etc.

Danny's father was murdered by a radical political group in Chicago. It was a case of mistaken identity. They bombed the wrong house. Danny holds no bitterness. It takes a real man to be that way. I could never do that. He realizes that England did many terrible things to the Irish. However, he also feels that sometime we have to let the bitterness and hatred end. He will not allow anything political at his festivals.

I have not seen Danny since before Katrina struck. He lost both his pub and his home. However, we do talk on the phone. He put music to "Katrina's Angels". One of these days we will see each other and hang out for a while.

Danny had a wonderful Irish pub in the heart of the French Quarter until Hurricane Katrina. It was situated in a beautiful old building dating back to the 1700s. While I don't drink, I spent many hours there either talking with Danny, or listening to some wonderful music. Through Danny I met, and became friends with some great singers and musicians. I will truly miss my home away from home, O'Flaherty's Irish Channel Pub.

Danny' "A Man I Admire" is for you. Thank you for being such a good friend and such a good person. You are someone I can look up to.

In April 2008, Danny was in Boston. He had come to New England to participate in a Convention for Exceptional Children. I drove to Boston and we were able to get together and hang out for an evening. It was hard to believe that nearly three years had passed since we had last seen each other. We talked about New Orleans, our feelings about the city and what Katrina had done. It was great seeing him.

A Man I Admire

There's a man I admire more than others I know
A kind man and sensitive, though moody at times,
He feels deeply and cares for customs of long ago,
Pride in our heritage is always foremost in his mind.

A man of today, but still he will dwell in the past
Only to bring that past to life in the minds of others
With songs and stories he'll share knowledge vast
To enrich the lives of his Celtic sisters and brothers.

With the use of electronics, computers, and yes the TV
Comes the passing of music, visiting, and even folklore
Traditions that made one's culture rich cease to be.
He will tell you how our ancestors lived in days of yore.

Two men have had a great impact on me. One was my dad.
The other is a great friend with qualities I wish I had.
Compassion for others, including those who murdered his dad
Make me admire this man; a great friend in good times and bad.

Danny O'Flaherty came from the shores of auld Erin.
He writes music, sings songs, and tells stories; a real bard.
He is also a man of vast historical knowledge, but overall
His integrity and honesty make me proud to be Danny's friend.

Photo of Danny O'Flaherty on previous page
from author's collection.

Geri Johnson, Danny O'Flaherty and author.
From author's collection.

Shortly after I returned to Massachusetts, following Hurricane Katrina, at the end of September 2005, I attended a job fair. I stopped at one of the booths and learned about CareerPoint, a one-stop career center located in Holyoke Massachusetts. I had never been without a job and didn't know that the old unemployment offices had been replaced by one-stop career centers. This was one of the luckiest days of my life, close behind getting out of New Orleans. The entire staff at CareerPoint, from the executive director to the receptionists at the front desk, does everything possible to assist their clients. I can never thank them enough for all they did for me. In an attempt to express my gratitude to the wonderful people at CareerPoint I wrote a poem called "CareerPoint".

There was a one-stop career center about ten minutes from where I was staying, but I opted to drive the extra thirty miles so I could work with those marvelous professionals in Holyoke. The following poem is dedicated to the entire staff at CareerPoint with much love and gratitude. Thank you, CareerPoint.

CareerPoint

What is CareerPoint? What does it mean?
It's more than a building of brick and steel.
It's more than a name on a sign by the street.
It's caring, loving people who make it real.

CareerPoint is more than the sum of its parts.
Computers and counseling, workshops and then
Professionals from various fields practice their arts
To assist the unemployed become productive again.

CareerPoint means help and hope, also a friend
To assist coping with job loss and all that strife,
Ex-offenders and dropouts are welcome to attend.
The goal is to help everyone start a new life.

It's okay to be discouraged. It comes with the turf.
The staff will make sure it doesn't become too great.
They'll guide you and help you, suggestions they'll offer
And before you know it, much progress you'll make.

If Katrina's the worst to ever happen to me,
Then CareerPoint is among the very best.
My task, to seek work to get back on my feet
And the fine folks at CareerPoint saw to the rest.

CareerPoint means many things, but at the top of the list
Are people who want to help others get a fresh start.
You are real heroes and I just want to say, "God Love
You all and I thank you from the bottom of my heart."

I attended a wedding this summer (2006). The bride was my second cousin. Her father and I had grown up together. After the ceremony, there were a few hours to kill before the reception. I decided to put my time to good use and employ my newfound talent to write a poem to honor the occasion. Several revisions later, "Hanna and Mike's Wedding" is ready to put in a frame and present to the Bride and Groom.

As I said, Hanna's father, John and I had grown up together. We had talked about going to New Orleans to retrieve my property, and the plans were finalized on the day of the wedding. Three weeks after the wedding, we were making our trek south.

Hanna And Mike's Wedding

On July 15, 2006, Hanna and Mike were wed.
When they exchanged their vows of fidelity and love
Two lives became one and a new family was started.
May God bless this holy union from heaven above.

St. Mary's Church was filled with family and friends,
There to see this happy couple become man and wife.
Wishing them well; blessings and joy without end
And witness Hanna and Mike begin their new life.

Friends and relations wishing the best,
For this new family that began today,
Watched as the marriage was blessed
By Fr. Bernier on this most joyous day.

Hanna and Mike begin their new life
Surrounded by friends and loved ones.
We all wish that as the years go on
Your family is healthy and free from strife.

As you travel your married life together
And practice your vows of fidelity and love,
All life's storms, you'll be able to weather.
God will bless this holy union from heaven above.

Much of New Orleans covered with oily
floodwaters 9-05-05.
Photo courtesy of NOAA,
National Oceanic and Atmospheric Administration.

When I left New Orleans August 31, 2005, I had no idea if my apartment or even my furnishings had survived Hurricane Katrina. All I knew was that my two cats and I had survived and I was eternally grateful for that. Being a dreamer, I could only hope that my property was okay until I learned otherwise. Less than two weeks after Katrina struck, I talked with a FEMA inspector who told me that while she could not remember my apartment building, my street had flooding to first floor apartments. I lived on the third floor, so I knew I did not get flooded out. She also told me that some buildings had their roofs completely blown off. My property was not damaged by flood waters (that was the good news). But it might have been ruined by water that entered through a missing roof (that was the bad news).

I stayed with my in-laws in Houston for a couple of weeks and then we started for Massachusetts. Jefferson Parish was still closed. Residents were only allowed to go to their homes to take some pictures and collect a few essentials and then they had to leave. It made no sense to drive for several hours to grab a few things that might or might not be there, and then drive for several more hours before I could find a place to sleep. I decided to head for Massachusetts, where I was born and raised and try to start over.

In October, I talked with the apartment management people who told me that my apartment was not ruined, but they could not remember how much damage there was to my belongings.

I was finally able to return to New Orleans in early August 2006, nearly a year after Katrina struck. A whole bag of mixed emotions accompanied me. As we got closer to Louisiana they became stronger. About a hundred miles out, the emotions became much more intense as more evidence of the destruction became visible. Broken trees, signs knocked down, steel bent and twisted as though some deranged giant pretzel maker shaped steel beams like he would his dough. Traveling from Slidell to New Orleans I could see where Interstate 10 bridges had been lifted off their abutments by the storm surge and had been temporarily repaired. Driving through New Orleans East brought tears to my eyes. Seeing mile after mile of apartments and homes that had been completely destroyed made me think of the wonderful, elderly, black couple I had met in Houston and that dear, sweet lady who had lost everything, and who said to me, "I think you need a hug." I regret that I never got your names, but I think of you often and I wish you well.

I lost some property, but I was able to salvage most of it. After being without it for a year, and considering that many people lost everything, I would have felt lucky if I had only saved one item. I got to see old friends, which was very healing. While I would not wish Katrina on anyone, I thank God I got to experience it. It caused me to change my life for the better. "Going Back" is an attempt to share with you the emotions I felt going back to New Orleans. I hope I succeeded.

Going Back

Fear, unease, trepidation, anxiety,
Elation, happiness, pleasure, joy
All emotions building faster and faster
When returning to the scene of the disaster.

Seeing the carnage brought tears to my eyes.
My heart ached for my fellow man's loss,
New Orleans East a ghost town under sunny skies,
A year after Katrina proved nature was boss.

The Lower Ninth Ward and even downtown,
Devastation and wreckage like an open sore,
Another hurricane season and the city's not ready.
Please God, spare her, she can't take any more.

Seeing old friends was just like medicine to me.
I came back to retrieve my clothes and things,
But I left with much more than I owned
Big Easy people lost so much but are still giving.

I returned to New Orleans with mixed feelings.
The city, though severely wounded is still alive.
Though I cried and felt pain, I did much healing
Thanks to Katrina's Angels who continue to thrive.

Kind, loving people make up the heart of New Orleans.
Though they lost so very much, they continue to give.
It will take years to rebuild, but their spirit means
That a better New Orleans will persevere and live.

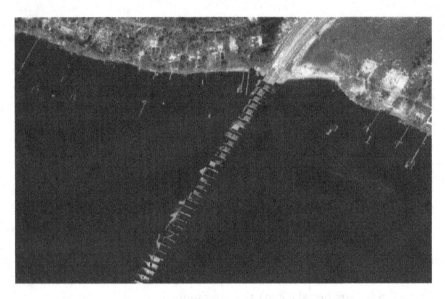

New Orleans Bridge roadway washed
away by storm surge.
Photo courtesy of NOAA.

When I first read that New Orleans was going to celebrate Mardi Gras just months after Hurricane Katrina devastated the Mississippi Gulf Coast, I had very mixed feelings. I couldn't decide if it was a good thing or not. How could a city that had just gone through near total destruction brought on by Hurricane Katrina and all the suffering it caused, hold its colossal party? I finally realized that New Orleans, as well as other devastated areas needed some normalcy to cope with the disaster.

I returned to New Orleans in August 2006, nearly a year after Katrina struck. When I saw the condition of the city and talked with people who lost so much, I realized a city must be rebuilt in the same manner that it was originally constructed. If you build a thousand houses with no business, no one will live in them because there are no jobs. If you open a hundred stores with no houses, there will be no customers. You need a careful blend of both.

During my visit, I learned that on Sept. 25, 2006, the New Orleans Saints were going to play their first game in the Superdome since Hurricane Katrina. Saints fans would be spending their money in New Orleans instead of some other city hosting the Saints 'home games'. All of their 2005 'home games' were played in other cities. What a boost this should be for the city! When I lived in the city, I was not a Saints fan. I guess I was just being an obnoxious Yankee. Since Katrina, I have become an ardent Saints fan. I think it's part of my love and longing for the city that holds my heart.

I remember going up to the roof of the hotel where I was based and looking around after the storm. About four blocks away, as the crow flies, was the Superdome. Its roof had been peeled back like a giant orange. Thousands of people had sought refuge there and during the height of the storm, the Dome lost its roof. How terrifying it must have been for those wretched people! They were to remain there for several more days with no power, no food, no water, and no sanitation, with the floodwaters rising. I will never forget my last look at the Dome before leaving the city. Nor will I ever forget the television pictures of the people in the Superdome.

The images of pain and suffering are as clear in my mind today, as they were back in August 2005.

When I turned on the television that September evening, I saw thousands of happy, cheering people in the Superdome. What a contrast that was to my last images of the New Orleans Superdome. I immediately grabbed a pad and pen and began to take notes for my next poem. "A Football Game" shows that contrast along with the hope for the city's recovery.

A Football Game

Millions saw the New Orleans Superdome packed
With thousands of suffering and dying souls.
All hope gone as they huddled in fear and despair,
Their pleas and tears seen by people around the world.

Fifty-six weeks later.

Millions saw the New Orleans Superdome packed
With thousands of joyous and hopeful souls.
The city still lay in rubble and their homes were gone,
But the Saints had returned; a symbol of renewed hope.

Could a football game erase all the suffering and pain?
Ninety seconds into the game a fumble and the Saints score!
During the next three quarters, more points they scored.
The event at the Superdome was more than a football game.

People without homes went to watch the Saints play that night.
For about four hours they were able to put their troubles aside.
They laughed and smiled and cheered them with all their might.
The past thirteen months for just a little while was left behind.

Much more than a contest, this football game of the century
The fact that the Saints won only added to its total importance,
Its real significance is the world saw a step in the city's recovery.
A giant step as big business began to return to New Orleans.

Restoring this once magnificent city to its former grandeur
Which at first glance appears to be a monumental endeavor,
Will be accomplished one convention, football game or
Cruise at a time as New Orleans continues to rebuild.

Those of us who were there in the aftermath of Katrina
Will never forget the sight and sound of suffering and horror.
But we must look forward with renewed hope as the
Tourists return and the economy continues to recover.

New Orleans Superdome with most
of its roof gone.
Photo courtesy of NOAA.

During the summer of 2007, I decided that I needed to take a vacation. I wanted to get away and relax, but I also wanted to do some writing. I had some ideas for poems, but I felt stymied and unable to write. What I did do however, was to take copious notes about what I wanted to write. I then made a 'projects' list of what I wanted to write about. I made a reservation at the Sea Cliff Inn in Old Orchard Beach, Maine for Nov 3 – 10. I had the Penthouse which was a delightful room on the third floor, with a beautiful ocean view.

The way up to the Penthouse at the Sea Cliff Inn is via a steep, narrow, outside staircase. There is no elevator. This is important to note because a week before I was to leave for my vacation, my used laptop would not start up. There was no way I could get it repaired before I left. Since I didn't have my laptop, and I wanted to do some writing, I took my whole blooming computer; tower, monitor, keyboard, mouse, speakers, along with all the wires. Did I mention that the room was on the third floor and there was no elevator?

I set a goal of seven poems to write that week. As the second anniversary of Hurricane Katrina approached and the memories returned, I made many notes. During that period, I thought that if my parents had not taught me how to fight adversity, I might not have made it through Katrina and its aftermath, and I never thanked them for all they did. I thought of how our environment had been damaged so badly by Katrina, but nowhere as severely as it has been by our automobiles and factories. Lake Pontchartrain had been polluted so badly over the years that it was unsafe for swimming. It took twenty years to clean it and in 2005, it was deemed to be safe for swimming once again. After Katrina, all the floodwater was pumped out of New Orleans into Lake Pontchartrain. All that poison back into the lake! How long will it take to clean this time? This was good for two poems, "Ocean" and "Our Body".

I never realized that I had a talent for writing poetry until after Hurricane Katrina. Perhaps, I still don't. When I wrote "Katrina's Angels", it was an attempt to thank all those wonderful people who helped me, and all the other victims of the great disaster. Over the next two years, I wrote a couple dozen poems. They dealt with Katrina, its effect on me and the changes it brought about in my life.

While I think of my parents often, I am ashamed to say that I never thought about writing about them until recently (2007). A good friend of mine, singer and songwriter, Danny O'Flaherty wrote a song called "I Didn't Get A Chance". He never got a chance to tell his father that he loved him before he died.

We always feel that there will be time, or else we fail to think to say the important things before we lose someone. In my case, I told my parents that I loved them, but I never took the time to thank them. They gave me so very much and I just took it for granted. I regret that very much. "My Parents" is an attempt to do just that, to say, "Thank you, Mom and Dad." Rest in peace. Love, Jack.

My Parents

My parents were simple first and second generation Irish.
They worked very hard all their lives and raised two sons.
One child was very sickly and the other (me) was a hellion.
I received a college education and fulfilled their greatest wish.

It's true they were never able to finish high school
But my father was the smartest man I ever knew.
And my mother with her wisdom; certainly was no fool.
Through observation and reading, their knowledge grew.

They worked hard and showered us with great love.
We got most of the material things we asked for
But most of all, their loving example and guidance
Made our happy home the greatest treasure trove.

With much patience and great parental love,
You taught the difference between right and wrong.
A gentle hand to guide us on the right path
To live the golden rule and avoid God's wrath.

Mom and Dad, you are both gone now,
Thirty-five years for Dad, Mom twelve years for you.
While I gave you both all your gray hairs, you knew
I loved you, but I never did get to say, "Thank you."

I have always loved being near the ocean. Whenever I'm near the ocean, I have to get in the water. It doesn't matter the time of year. Now, I may be crazy, but I'm not stupid (although I'm sure I could get an argument there!). In the cold weather, I make sure my torso is covered with a heavy fisherman's knit sweater. I will only go in up to my thighs. I am also aware of hypothermia, so no matter how good the water feels, I won't stay in for more than a few minutes. Then it's back to the room for a hot shower.

I love the seashore. Whenever I'm there, I have the window open all night so I can hear the waves breaking on the beach. Summer or winter the sound lulls me into a deep, restful sleep. I wake up in the morning with a clear head feeling completely refreshed.

I look forward to the day when we finally stop polluting our oceans and begin using them to their full potential. We are depleting our supply of certain species of fish by over-fishing. Good resource management can reverse that trend. Aquaculture technology could feed much of the world's population. I also look at the constant motion of the ocean and wonder why we can't harness that endless energy to supply our electrical needs. Why can't we use that energy to light our cities and heat our homes? Along with wind and solar, here is another endless source of renewable energy that does not pollute the atmosphere. Can this be another way to end our dependence on fossil fuel?

Ocean

The waves break continuously on the shore,
Some with a gentle murmur, others a loud roar.
The soothing sound, while constantly in motion,
The peaceful, yet sometimes mighty ocean.

Water so blue or green, or when angry, gray;
The source of life, and also the cause of death.
Millions depend on your bounty each day,
While many thousands flee from your wrath.

Constant motion could possibly mean
Endless power to light our cities and towns,
Heat our homes. Learn how to do it man
While there is still time to keep our planet green.

For me the ocean means beauty and serenity.
At night it lulls me into a deep, restful sleep.
I also ask why the ocean can't be used as a clean,
Renewable source to satisfy our needs for electricity?

The waves break continuously on the shore.
Some with a gentle murmur, others a loud roar.
This huge body of water constantly in motion
Can we really find our salvation in the ocean?

Old Orchard Beach, Maine
From author's collection.

I smoked heavily for about thirty-one years. I also drank heavily for many years. I have been free of alcohol for over twenty-three years and free of tobacco for over twenty-one years. I should have many illnesses from this abuse my body suffered. I am very happy to say the only lasting effect from smoking is some cardio-vascular disease. While I don't treat this lightly, it could have been a lot more serious. I consider myself to be extremely lucky. Against tremendous odds, my body repaired itself almost completely.

I have a great deal of anger with our government. I don't advocate a lot of government intervention, but I do believe it is necessary in some areas. Our air and water are poisoned; the atmosphere damaged because the government will not regulate big business, mostly oil. Tobacco does nothing but kill, but it is still legal because of the money involved.

Gun manufacturers have been sued by government, the city of New Orleans stating that guns kill people. The city was attempting to obtain a settlement similar to the tobacco settlement. The suit was eventually dismissed. I will not enter that argument. However, I will state that millions of gun owners have used guns for the purpose they were designed, and no one was killed. If cigarettes are used for the purpose they were designed, there is only one result. People die! Yet the government will not ban tobacco. I have heard that agriculture will suffer if tobacco is banned. Why can't that land be used to grow crops such as corn to be used to make a non-food quality vegetable oil to be used to power motor vehicles? That would not only help the economy of agriculture, it would also help the economy in general with lower fuel prices. It would also help to reduce our ever-growing dependence on foreign oil. In addition, this bio-diesel fuel would produce fewer pollutants. The result would be cleaner air, a cleaner atmosphere and a large reduction in greenhouse gasses. We would also have a much healthier population.

Our bodies do an amazing job of healing themselves and regenerating tissue. Traditional wisdom held that the body could regenerate all tissue except nerve tissue. Science has learned how to help the body rebuild damaged nerve tissue also. It's only a matter of time before doctors learn how to repair spinal cord injuries so they no longer paralyze people. Imagine how well our bodies would work in a clean environment with today's medicine. I wrote "Our Body" because I am amazed at how well our bodies serve us in spite of the abuse we give them.

Our Body

Fast food, cigarettes, illegal drugs and booze
Poured in our bodies, as a poor lifestyle we choose.
In our youth we fail to consider the consequences,
The damage caused before we come to our senses.

Our bodies work like magnificent machines.
They process the toxins we so eagerly consume.
Trying to rebuild tissue to make our body clean
In order that a healthy existence we can resume.

We mistreat our bodies with so much abuse,
Unhealthy lifestyles, so many poor choices,
Year after year of ill treatment and misuse,
Yet they continue to give us decades of use.

Our bodies continue to wage an unfair fight
Against society, the environment, companies,
Government, big business, greedy people,
All with only the almighty dollar in sight.

A truly marvelous piece of engineering
The human body. Imagine what would be
The result if we were to stop the poisoning;
And treated our bodies respectfully.

I-10 underwater in downtown
New Orleans 10-08-05.
Photo courtesy of NOAA.

When I left New Orleans late in the afternoon of August 31, 2005, I was driving my old, beat up 1994 Pontiac Bonneville. The car had over 220,000 miles on it, and had floodwater sloshing around on the floorboards. I also had my two cats and the clothes on my back. My tee shirt and shorts were oil stained, and my sneakers were wet and oil soaked. As I was leaving this ravaged city, I knew that I was a wealthy man.

There is a book titled "Live Like You Were Dying" written by Michael Morris. Tim McGraw sang the song of the same title. It's about someone who develops a potentially life threatening illness and how he comes to realize that things he considered important really meant nothing. He refocuses on the truly important things and becomes a much happier person for it. When I first heard "Live Like You Were Dying", and then read the book, I adopted its message. While I did not have a potentially life threatening illness, I came as close to dying from Katrina, as I ever want, until the real thing comes along. I do hope everyone gets to live like they were dying, then they will find what really matters.

The happiest time in my life was in the spring of 2006. I had moved to New England and found a job. I got a huge four-room apartment. My bedroom set consisted of a borrowed bed and dresser. My dining room set was a folding TV table and a folding metal chair. My pride and joy was my living room suite. I had bought a new television. The TV stand was the box it came in and I had an aluminum lawn chair. What more could I have asked for? Somewhere along the line, I had 'learned' that a person needed to acquire 'things' to be happy in life. Katrina taught me you do not need material things to be happy. I was beginning to rebuild my life.

In the winter of 2007, I became quite ill. As the illness dragged on for months and I got sicker, I decided that when I got well, I had to write "Our Greatest Possession". I finally had a colonoscopy, an endoscopy and a CT scan. The diagnosis was a diverticular abscess. Four months later, I had another CT scan. It showed the infected area was smaller and surgery was not needed. I also received more good news. It was not cancerous! I am on my way to regaining my greatest possession, my health. Sometimes it's hard to remember that if we have our health, nothing else matters. But it is so true. Our health really is our greatest possession.

Our Greatest Possession

Throughout our lives we amass many things.
We work very hard to earn enough money
To buy homes, cars, clothes, watches and rings.
Our vision clouds as we think all is sunny.

We buy fine things for our loving spouses.
We strive to raise our kids with comfort and love,
Giving them nice things and fine houses.
Hard work pays off; blest by God above.

Others struggle their whole lives through
In vain attempts to achieve the American Dream.
They never manage to accumulate more than a few
Dollars as they fail in scheme after scheme.

"Live Like You Were Dying" says it all.
For all our endeavors only one thing matters,
It's not the material things. If we never learn
To live like we were dying, then we all fail.

After Hurricane Katrina, I left New Orleans
With nothing more than the clothes on my back,
But I knew that I possessed such great wealth,
I learned that I had the greatest possession..........
my health!

After the attacks of September 11, 2001, people from around the country rushed to help the people of New York and the other victims in Washington, DC and Pennsylvania. The love and kindness of ordinary citizens overshadowed the evil of the terrorists. People from Louisiana held fundraisers to raise enough money to build a fire engine. The money was raised and the fire truck was built in Louisiana. When it was completed, the "Spirit of Louisiana" was delivered to New York City and donated to the New York Fire Department.

People working for the Gumbo Company of New Orleans made several trips to New York to cook and serve hot gumbo and jambalaya to the rescue workers at Ground Zero during the bitter cold fall and winter months.

After Hurricane Katrina devastated New Orleans, New York City Police Officers and Firefighters were among the first volunteers to come to the city to help out. You remembered! Thank you!

You Remembered

The attack on the World Trade Center was a national disaster.
Planned and carried out by evil men; done in God's name.
Over three thousand people died in the unnatural disaster
But the goodness of humankind put the evildoers to shame.

People from around the country donated money and time
To try to ease the suffering and pain of the many victims
And their relatives and friends. Helping those who
Just happened to be in the wrong place at the wrong time.

The good people of Louisiana did their part to help.
They traveled to Ground Zero to cook and serve gumbo
And jambalaya to the rescue workers. The workers who
Toiled to save lives and recover bodies in the winter's bitter cold.

Louisianans collected donations, held fundraisers,
Conducted raffles and many other forms of charity
To build a fire truck pumper and when it was done,
Delivered the "Spirit of Louisiana" to New York City.

Four years later, a natural disaster nearly destroyed
New Orleans as it was shattered by Hurricane Katrina.
Police Officers and Firefighters from the Big Apple
Were among the first to rush to the Big Easy. You remembered!

As the second anniversary of Hurricane Katrina approached, emotions began welling up inside me. While I think about Katrina every day, the memories returned to haunt me. At first, I was alarmed that the memories were returning. Then I realized that this was a major event that played a huge role in my life. The memories and nightmares will always be there. As time has gone by, however, the nightmares are less frequent. The trick is to deal with them appropriately and not dwell on them. Also, deal with them and not try to suppress them.

It is with this goal in mind, that I wrote "Two Years Later". After two years, I have friends and acquaintances who I don't know if they are dead or alive. Others I know survived, but whom I have not been able to communicate with. There also those to whom I have talked, but have not seen since before Katrina struck. I have met many of Katrina's victims and families of Katrina's victims. Some stories have a happy ending, others do not.

We often talk about rebuilding New Orleans and the Gulf Coast, but once again the media has missed the important point. The human victims; People! "Two Years Later" is an attempt to bring them back to the forefront. Even though I don't know most of you, I will never forget you.

Two Years Later

Two years after Hurricane Katrina wreaked
Death and destruction on the Gulf Coast,
I pause to offer a prayer for her victims,
I also thank God that I was luckier than most.

Much of New Orleans still lies in ruins,
While other neighborhoods have been rebuilt.
All along the Gulf Coast rebuilding continues.
Many years will pass before the job is complete.

My mind now turns to the victims; the people.
How are you doing? Are things going well?
Or is it still a struggle? Have the nightmares
Ended? Or are you still living them in hell?

We hear about rebuilding the infrastructure,
But it's far more important to rebuild lives.
For many people's lives were changed forever.
Many will move on; some will never recover.

On the anniversary of that fateful date
My thoughts and emotions are running wild.
I remember the horror, also the kindness of man.
May God grant the victims comfort, the peace of a child.

Every year on the twenty-ninth of August,
I will reflect on the rebuilding progress.
I still also remember the other victims
And pray you are well into the healing process.

Rushing floodwaters consume New Orleans
as Katrina ravishes the city.
Photo courtesy of NOAA.

Over the years, I have done a lot of complaining about my life. God was unfair to me. Why couldn't I have what others had? Why couldn't I do what others have done? Why I couldn't I go places that other people go? On the rare occasions that I was completely honest with myself, I had to admit that things really were not that bad. Sure I had some tough knocks, but overall, life had been pretty good to me. However, that didn't fit in well with my negative attitude, so I would not let those thoughts last too long.

Hurricane Katrina gave me the chance to actually examine my life. I didn't like what I saw. I realized that I did not like myself very much. I didn't see much to like! I really was not a nice person. I was ungrateful and didn't appreciate the blessings I had received. My grumbling and complaining made me blind and unable to see those blessings. As a child, I used to see a priest on television, who would say, "It is better to light a candle than to curse the darkness." I did just that, I cursed the darkness.

I don't remember that priest's name, but his religious order was the Christopher's. His motto was, "If everyone lit just one candle, what a bright world this would be." As I look back, I realize that I had some rough spots, but they were nothing compared to the blessings I had received. As a police officer, I have done things that most people never dream of doing. I have been in burning buildings, pulled people out of wrecked cars, put criminals behind bars. I saw horrible pain and suffering, but I was also part of the process that helped repair some of the damage. I investigated accidents and crime scenes trying to piece together the events that led up to a tragedy. I also survived a major hurricane and flood, and have gone aerobatics flying. I have seen the worst and the best of humanity.

I have done things and experienced events that most people only read about. People with good imaginations may dream about doing some of the things they read in books, while I got to experience them every day. Most people only witness major protests and demonstrations on television. I got to talk with angry Viet Nam vets who would have liked nothing better than to string up 'Hanoi Jane', Jane Fonda with piano wire. While they were very angry, they assured me that they would not attack her since many of them were also police officers. They kept their word. I also got to talk with Abby Hoffman of the infamous 'Chicago Seven' and Amy Carter, former President Jimmie Carter's daughter, as we were transporting them to jail after arresting them during a protest. In addition, I got to lock up an idiot who threatened the life of Vice-Presidential candidate Geraldine Ferraro as she was campaigning at the University of Massachusetts.

In short, I have really lived life. I now thank God every day for the wonderful life I have had. I am lighting that candle. Who wants to join me and brighten up this world?

My life has been a pretty good ride.............So far!

So Far

I've been knocked down and battered by life.
Sometimes kicked so hard I felt I could not
Get back up and face any more grief and strife.
So easy to check out, to put an end to all this rot!

I've also received fortune and blessings untold,
Often too blind to see the treasure and wealth,
Unable to know there is more to riches than gold.
The greatest treasure of all is your health.

How often I complained that life was unfair.
Why couldn't I have what other people had?
As I look back, I was right. Life is not fair.
I've had more good fortune than most have had!

I've had experiences and done many things
Other people can only dream or read about.
They live their lives vicariously, never taking
A chance, too timid to dance, afraid to shout.

When I take the time to look back, I'm not sad.
I examine the tough times and the good times.
After a careful and honest inspection, I find
That I've had many more good times than bad.

When my time on this earth is over,
At the Pearly Gates, St. Peter will ask me
Where I want to go. I'll say it won't matter,
I want to try it all. It's been a pretty good ride........
                                                So far!

Another section of New Orleans
underwater with the CBD in background.
Photo courtesy of NOAA.

Fate or Destiny, or whatever name it goes by is a very strange thing. Our hotel family left hurricane ravaged New Orleans in a six-car caravan, late in the afternoon on August 31, 2005. The plan was simple; go to Baton Rouge. The execution of this simple plan was difficult. We could not go west on Interstate 10 because I-10 west of New Orleans no longer existed. There was only one way in and out of New Orleans, and that was to cross the Mississippi River via the Crescent City Connection, two huge bridges spanning the river. These bridges were not affected by the storm surge because they were so high. Ocean liners pass under these structures. Once on the West Bank, the plan was to travel west on Highway 90 to I-310. We were to take I-310 to I-10 west, beyond the destroyed portion of the highway to Baton Rouge. This is where Fate showed its funny, little head.

Mine, was the sixth car in a six-car caravan. I watched the other five cars drive past the turn for I-310. I was the only Yankee in the caravan. I was also the only one who knew we were going the wrong way. When we got to Houma, we stopped for gas and I asked where we were going. I was told we were going to Baton Rouge and we would be taking the Sunset Bridge to get there. We started off again and drove to Morgan City. We were now in southwest Louisiana while Baton Rouge would be more to our northeast. When I asked again, I was once again told we were heading for Baton Rouge. Around 11:00PM we were in Lafayette, Louisiana, which is in the far western portion of the state. We stopped once more and I informed the group that I could not go any further. I had been up since 8:00PM the night before and I was exhausted. The entrance to I-10 was right there and they were going to get on and drive to Baton Rouge. We bid our farewells and wished each other well.

At that time, I was in shock and suffering from chemical burns so I was not thinking very clearly myself. I don't want to sound like I'm criticizing my hotel family. I love those people, but I've never seen any of them since that night. We had been through a whole lot together and they were probably not in any better shape than I was. I have never been able to figure why we wound up in Lafayette when we were heading for Baton

Rouge, but I'm not complaining. I find some humor in a tragic situation. I also find the irony of Fate to be so great!

I decided that I would stay in Lafayette that night and decide where to go after I had rested and had a good night's sleep. I found a WalMart and bought some tee shirts, shorts and sneakers for myself. I also bought some food, bowls and a litter box and some litter for the cats. I realized that they must be hungry and probably would like to relieve themselves since they had been in their carriers since early morning. One of the things that amazed me about our exodus was that these two cats never made a peep all day. They must have sensed that something enormous had occurred, and was still going on. By just traveling and not squawking, they kept a lot of pressure off me. I didn't have to worry about them, even though I knew they would need attention at some point.

After shopping for the necessities, I looked for a motel. It was then that I got my first hint that Fate had played a role, although I didn't have a clue what the role was. I learned that we would not be able to get a room until we got to Texas. I got some gas and found a pay phone. I was able to call my daughter and leave a message on her voice mail. For three days, no one knew if I was dead or alive since there was no phone service in New Orleans. As a matter of fact, my cell phone did not have any service in New Orleans Sunday evening and the hurricane never arrived until Monday morning.

As an aside, I learned on February 24, 2010, while trying to obtain some replacement shares of stock that were lost during Katrina, that I am deceased. That was a bit of a shock to me since I was talking to people on the phone at the time, when they told me that I was dead. They said that since I was dead, they could not help me on the phone, because I must be an imposter. They told me that I would have to write them a letter. On the phone, I must be an imposter since I'm dead, but in a letter, I'm really me and I'm alive! Mind boggling! I knew that I was reported missing after Katrina, but I didn't realize that I had died until Feb. 24.

Early in the morning (August 31, 2005) I had fed the cats and then put them in their carriers in anticipation of evacuating the hotel. The evacuation had been delayed and wasn't completed until late afternoon. We managers had met in the Command Center at 6:00AM. We ate breakfast of white bread and bottled water. Believe it or not, it tasted pretty good! I wasn't going to eat again until I could feed the cats. They were completely dependent on me to feed them. They seemed to sense that we were escaping because they never made a sound during our exodus. I was able to give

80

them some water during one of our stops. However, when I discovered that I had another five or six hours of driving ahead of me, I knew I needed some nourishment, especially some coffee. Around 12:30 or 1:00AM on Thursday morning, I found a Waffle House. I went in and ordered some pork chops and eggs. I have never had pork chops and eggs before or since that night. However, since it was the first hot food I had eaten since the previous Saturday, it tasted great!

When I returned to the car after eating, the windows were all fogged up from the water-soaked carpeting. I had to run the defroster for several minutes and open the windows to clear them. Even though it was hot and muggy, I had to leave the windows open and run the defroster every time I stopped for more than a couple of minutes. This was a minor inconvenience and when I realized that thousands of cars had been trapped under water, I felt very lucky indeed.

We finally got to a motel in Houston at 5:00AM. Since it was Labor Day weekend, the motel was booked. I would have to leave the motel on Friday. I talked with my daughter later on that morning so everyone at home knew that I had survived Hurricane Katrina. I located a AAA office not too far from the motel. I asked them to prepare a TripTik for me. They told me that they would have it ready for me on Tuesday. When I explained my situation to them, they told me to pick it up at 1:00PM. Late-morning the phone in my room rang. I just knew it was my ex-wife whom I had tried to hate for seven years. When I heard the genuine concern in her voice, all animosity was gone. I also learned that I was able to give the forgiveness that I had been withholding for several years. She reminded me that her brother and his wife lived in Houston and they wanted me to stay with them. By the time I had returned from picking up my TripTik, my sister-in-law had called the motel and left a message for me to call her back.

I returned Linda's call and she told me how happy they were to learn that I had survived and had come to Houston. She gave me directions to their house. She then told me that she had seen a newspaper article about doctors who were seeing Katrina victims for free, if they didn't have insurance. She had made an appointment for me to see one the next day.

That evening, I heard from other of my in-laws who also offered me a place to stay. I still consider these people my in-laws, as several of them have said, "She divorced you; we didn't." I thank them all for their support and love during a very difficult time in my life.

81

If Fate hadn't sent me to Houston, instead of Baton Rouge, I'm not sure what would have happened, but I know it would not have been as good as it was in Texas. I would not have experienced the kindness that I received from the Katrina's Angels of Texas. Thank you, Texas, and God love y'all.

Texas

I've always had fond memories of the Lone Star State.
But none as sweet as those after Hurricane Katrina struck.
Arriving as refugees, you welcomed us with such great
Love, we knew there would be a change in our luck.

The orders of the day were acts of kindness large and small,
Individuals and businesses reaching out to sisters and brothers,
Giving great comfort, succor and assistance to one and all
Showed Texans' great compassion and concern for others.

Businesses, doctors, veterinarians, restaurants all giving
Free services or discounts to Katrina's wretched survivors.
By busloads they poured into your cities, some barely living.
You housed them and fed them and became real saviors.

Everywhere, signs offering discounts and words of comfort.
Companies and people collecting money, clothing and food,
Churches and parishioners offering hot meals and shelter
Welcoming poor strangers into their hearts and neighborhood.

There are not many things bigger than the state of Texas.
Many entire countries are nowhere as large as you are.
I've found one thing larger than Texas in my travels near and far.
That's the enormous heart of the wonderful people of Texas.
Thank you.

Rescue boats in New Orleans
Photo Courtesy of NOAA.

During November of 2007, I was talking with a friend of mine, Sarah Etelman. We were discussing our plans for the upcoming Thanksgiving holiday. The discussion turned to the meaning of Thanksgiving. That discussion led to my writing "True Meanings". Thanks for the inspiration, Sarah.

When I was a kid, my parents celebrated the holidays pretty much the way they were meant to be celebrated. We attended the Memorial Day Parade. Then we would all pile in the car and visit the cemeteries where our relatives were buried. November 11 was Armistice Day commemorating the end of World War I. Thanksgiving was a time for family. My aunt was always at our house for our feast. However, there was always a part of the day set aside to be thankful for our blessings.

When I got married for the second time, Thanksgiving was held at our house. My father had passed away several years earlier, but my mother, my two daughters, my brother, my wife's parents, her sister and her husband all came to our house for our feast. Somewhere along the line, I forgot to be grateful, but I carried on the rest of the tradition. After my wife left me, I moved to New Orleans. Thanksgiving became a lonely day, but I figured if I got a turkey dinner, I could celebrate Thanksgiving on a small scale.

While I was in New Orleans, my children, who were grown up, developed their own ways to celebrate the holiday. After Hurricane Katrina, I returned to Massachusetts. At first I was very disappointed that we were not going to be together on Thanksgiving. I started to feel sorry for myself. Then I asked if Katrina hadn't taught me anything. I realized that while it might be comforting to be with family on the holiday, it's not what Thanksgiving is all about. I went to the Salvation Army and offered my services to help others, less fortunate, have a good holiday meal. For the past four years, I have delivered Thanksgiving dinners to shut-ins. It is a tradition, I intend to continue. Doing something for others, who are less fortunate than I am, is my way of expressing my gratitude for the blessings I have received. It is also my way of paying it forward.

After Hurricane Katrina, when I was staying with my brother-in- law and his wife, I said that I could never pay them back for all they had done for me. Linda said, "Don't try to pay it back. Pay it forward."

True Meanings

Throughout the year we celebrate our national holidays
With trips, barbeques, bright lights, gifts and great feasts,
Parades, fireworks, parties, huge sales, plus many other ways
But how many of us remember what each holiday really means?

Whether religious, patriotic or born of some other origin
Our holidays have become commercial, their meanings forgotten.
Select a holiday and then tell me, "How did it begin?"
A simple task? Yes, but for how many people out of ten?

Memorial Day is the unofficial start of the summer season.
Veteran's Day is a time for a sale. Buy more and save!
A great time for a picnic or shopping. No time for soldiers
And sailors who gave so much, many lying in their graves.

Thanksgiving is to buy food and prepare a great feast.
Turkeys, potatoes, squash, cranberries from the bog,
Gather family and friends and eat like a starving hog.
Not a time to thank God for the blessings we receive.

Christmas is for shopping, parties and colored lights.
Be politically correct and wish "Happy Holidays",
The etiquette for re-gifting takes us to new 'heights'
To hell with brotherly love and peace on earth!

Semi-trailers tossed around
like matchsticks by Katrina.
Photo courtesy of NOAA.

I lived in New Orleans for about seven years. While it was not my best move, financially, I thoroughly enjoyed my time in the city. I loved the history, culture, and artistic atmosphere of the French Quarter. One can actually feel the artistic energy while strolling through the streets of the Vieux Carré. I also made some good friends in New Orleans. Since leaving the city three days after Katrina, I have realized that I have a great love for the 'Big Easy'. I can never live there again, because I can never go through another hurricane. After I left, I developed a pretty good case of 'survivor's guilt'. I knew from the get-go that this was irrational, but it was there and it was real. I have learned pretty much to deal with it and I think my writings help. If nothing else, they call attention to the victims of Hurricane Katrina.

Having said all that, the purpose for writing "Gratitude" is to thank all the unsung heroes of this great tragedy. People from all walks of life and of all social status went to New Orleans to help with the recovery. As a University Police Officer, I became very cynical and wondered about the future of our country. It's very easy to forget that you are only dealing with a small minority of college students who cause problems. When I saw the numbers of college students who gave up their spring break of constant booze and parties to come to the Gulf Coast to help Katrina's victims, I knew there was a bright future for our country. There are also high school students, civic organizations and church groups that are still helping in the Gulf Coast.

Many other people have given up well earned vacation time to go to the disaster scene to work hard to assist their fellow man. A number of them have traveled at their own expense just to help someone in need. More often than not, they did not have friends or relatives there; they just had a need to help someone less fortunate than themselves.

Every time I meet someone who has either gone down to the Gulf Coast to help, or who is going, I make it a point to thank them. Leslie, a counselor at CareerPoint and Robin McGuffey, my dental hygienist have both gone down with their respective churches. I have thanked both of them personally. People like you give more than you will ever realize to those who have just lost so very much.

To all of you, I offer my sincere thanks. I love you all and will always hold you close to my heart, even though I will never meet most of you. To all you wonderful people, I dedicate "Gratitude".

Gratitude

College students going on a drunken spree
The only true way to spend Spring Break.
No Sir! These people went to New Orleans
To help fix the damage Katrina did wreak.

Civic groups and churches have sent legions
To the Gulf Coast to help the recovery effort.
Nearly three years later, they still bring comfort
And assistance to the still suffering minions.

Young men and women, seniors, even teenagers
Helping to rebuild houses, clear the rubble and feed
Homeless victims. They ask for nothing in return
Because they are satisfying their own inner need.

You went in groups and you went on your own.
Taking time off from work and from school,
You left your families and friends back home
To help a complete stranger in some distant town.

You didn't ask for recognition or public thanks
But, when brothers and sisters were in great need
You joined others and helped close the ranks.
To all of you I offer my gratitude and thanks.

When I left New Orleans late in the afternoon of August 31, 2005, I had no idea how badly the city had been wounded. I had no idea that it would be nearly a full year before I could get back to retrieve my property. Over the next several days and weeks, I learned just how vast the destruction was to a city that I loved. As I watched television reports and read newspapers, I couldn't hold the tears back. Could this marvelous city recover, or had it suffered a mortal blow? How many of its buildings would have to be demolished if their bases remained in the floodwaters too long? What about its people? Would they have the stamina to rebuild?

As time went on, we learned that the city would be rebuilt. It will take years to rebuild, but the people do have the will and stamina to do the job. I hope I'm still alive to see the task completed.

Someone once said, "Home is where the heart is." There is a lot of truth in that statement. I now live in New Hampshire. I was born and raised in New England and moved back here after I left New Orleans. The main reason I moved back here is because there are no Category 5 hurricanes in New England. I can't go through another hurricane. Having said that, I do have to confess that my heart is in New Orleans. I'll have to content myself with an occasional visit. This is the reason that I wrote "Home".

Home

They say home is where the heart is.
I don't doubt that this is all very true.
Do you know what this really means?
My home is really in New Orleans.

While Katrina ravaged New Orleans
And I watched in fascinated wonder,
I only saw its power and wild fury
As it played out in a very small scene.

Over the following days and weeks,
When I saw the devastation t'was done,
Bitter tears flowed down my cheeks
As I saw the very soul torn from my home.

Three days after Katrina, I left my home.
New Orleans was gravely wounded
By wind and water, however,
Given time, I hope my home will recover.

My heart will always be in the Big Easy.
Even though I can never live there again,
I ask myself if I will ever see the day when
My home is returned to her former beauty?

Railroad cars are also tossed around
like so many matchsticks.
Photo courtesy of NOAA.

The spring and summer of 2008 was a very hectic time. Between work and things happening in my personal life, time seemed to fly by. In April, I finally got to see my very good friend, Danny O'Flaherty for the first time since July 2005. The reunion didn't seem like nearly three years had gone by since we last saw each other. That weekend, Danny was doing a concert in the Boston area. He asked me to perform one of my poems on stage with him. What an honor it was to be on stage with Danny! I read "Katrina's Angels". It awakened a desire in me to perform my works on stage. I have a story to tell.

The following month, I saw a couple of performances in a small theater in Brattleboro, VT. I spoke with the manager about booking the theater, but the available dates did not work out. In mid-August, I was in the Greenfield Public Library in Greenfield, MA, when I noticed that they had a meeting room I could book. The room was free, but I could not charge for the program. That was fine. I figured I could use it as a learning experience to see where my program needed fine tuning. There was not much time to let people know that I was putting on a program on the third anniversary of Hurricane Katrina. The turnout was a little disappointing! Counting me, there was a total of one person attending. I did use it as a learning experience though. The next time, I will make sure that I have a lot more lead time see that it is publicized thoroughly.

Time is a great healer. While the pain caused by Hurricane Katrina has eased and the nightmares are less frequent, I know they will always be there. That's okay. It was a major event in my life. My main concern is still for the victims of Hurricane Katrina. I think of them often and wish that they are all recovering. However, I know that many will never recover. For them, the nightmares and pain will always be present.

As I was writing "The Third Anniversary", my thoughts went from the victims to Katrina's Angels, many of whom are also Katrina's victims. Katrina's Angels are those wonderful people who did all they could to help others. Many of them had just lost everything, and yet did everything they could to help ease the pain of others. The media were there. Since they were more able to move around than I was, they must have seen more of

95

the goodness of mankind than I did, yet they refused to show it. They focused on the worst that man had to offer, and refused to report on the best. The media should be ashamed and disgraced, but I'm sure they don't care. Sensationalism and pain and suffering sell advertising!

The Third Anniversary

Katrina, three years have passed since you brought death
And destruction to the Gulf Coast and New Orleans.
Many wounds have healed, but others are of a depth
So great they will never heal by mere human means.

With greater destructive force than was unleashed
On Hiroshima or Nagasaki some sixty years prior
You decimated the Gulf Coast to say the least,
You did your best with wind, flood and even fire.

As I reflect back on the third anniversary of that
Fateful August day. I recall the suffering and pain.
Even though the passage of time has lessened them
The memories and nightmares will always remain.

My thoughts and prayers also go out to my fellow
Victims; especially those who were less fortunate.
God grant mercy to those who perished; strength
To those who struggle each day to get up and go.

Katrina, you did something you didn't consider,
Even though you brought out the worst in man,
You also brought out the best man has to offer,
Compassion, love and caring for his fellow man.

The media should wallow in disgrace and shame.
Greed made you neglect your duty to report news
Fully. You never showed people who had just
Lost everything helping others. Wallow in shame!

In the summer of 1998, I decided to take some ballroom dancing lessons. The instructor was also a licensed massage therapist. After the lessons ended, I began to get massages on a regular basis.

Over the years, we developed a friendship. When Katrina struck New Orleans, where I was living, she contacted my daughter to make sure I was alright. However, the phones were out and no one knew whether I was dead or alive for three days. When Cailin learned that I survived and was returning to Massachusetts, she told my daughter that she wanted to give me a free massage. Believe me my poor battered body needed it.

While I was in New Orleans, Cailin went back to school in Colorado and is a mental health counselor as well as a massage therapist. During the past four years, we shed a few tears together as I unloaded some of my burden on her, revealing how Katrina affected me.

As I said, we became friends over the years. In January 2008, she told me she was expecting a child. I watched her over the next few months and saw the changes in her. As her body changed with her growing child, I was once again struck by that wonderful glow that she, and all pregnant women have. All mothers-to-be have a wonderful and beautiful glow in their faces. "Motherhood" is for all expectant mothers, but was inspired and is especially dedicated to my very good friend, Cailin Reiken.

Motherhood

Of all the billions of things God has created,
Whether located on earth or far out in space,
To my thinking, nothing else can compare
To the radiance on an expectant mothers' face.

It doesn't matter if she began life as a beauty queen
Or a Plain Jane, when that new life begins to grow
Inside her body, beginning as a microscopic seed
Every mother-to-be face takes on that special glow.

As her chemistry changes and her body swells
She begins to develop a certain joie de vivre.
Her beauty increases 'cause she knows full well
That she is nourishing the infant beginning to live.

Perhaps the growing love for the unborn child,
Perhaps the changes both chemical and physical,
The beauty and aura surrounding these women
I feel are all part and parcel of the birth miracle.

God love and bless all you expectant mothers,
I pray that your children are all born healthy.
I wish you joy and happiness, a life without bother.
May you always enjoy your special beauty!

I first learned of the birth of Arcadia Reiken sometime in mid-August 2008. While my daughter and I were talking on the phone, she happened to mention that Cailin Reiken had given birth to a baby girl. I told her that I hadn't received the email. She said that she would send me a copy of hers. At that time I was trying to put together a program for the third anniversary of Hurricane Katrina. I had recently changed internet service providers and my email address had changed. Through a series of comedic errors, I never got the email announcement until Nov. 20, 2008. Both Cailin and my daughter had incorrect email addresses for me.

When I first learned of the birth, I knew I was going to write a poem. My daughter, Mary sent me the email on Nov. 20, 2008. Seeing the picture of a beautiful baby girl with her proud parents gave me the inspiration for the following poem, "Arcadia".

I wish my good friend Cailin and her husband, Rick belated congratulations on the birth of a beautiful daughter. I also wish much happiness and joy to their family. May they always be healthy and happy.

Arcadia

Hello Arcadia. What a beautiful name!
When I first learned the news of your birth
I had to sit down and write a poem to say,
"Hello, Precious One, welcome to earth."

On August 6, 2008, the world was enriched
When Arcadia, daughter of Cailin and Rick
Arrived for the onset of life's passage;
The start of an exciting and wonderful voyage.

Mommy and Daddy are proud of you for
You are their whole world; their pride and joy.
Listen to their wisdom and heed their guidance,
And life's marvelous journey you will enjoy.

As you grow, and run, and play, and learn,
You will discover the world is a wondrous place.
The more facts you gain, the more you'll yearn
For more knowledge to grow in wisdom and grace.

Arcadia, for you my greatest and fondest desire
Is that you thoroughly enjoy your life's journey.
Suffer little of life's pain, but enjoy its pleasure
And live your life in complete peace and serenity.

Mile after mile of New Orleans
underwater.
Photo courtesy of NOAA.

In July 2009, the Cambridge, Massachusetts Police Department responded to a reported possible breaking and entering into a home. The caller reported that two men appeared to be forcing their way into the residence. It was a local routine call that should have remained local, but it became national and even international.

Harvard Professor Henry Louis Gates, who is black, reportedly refused to show his identification when the Cambridge Police arrived on the scene and found him in the house. Professor Gates was eventually arrested for disorderly conduct. He accused the officer, Sgt. James Crowley of being a racist and the incident took off from there. The charges against Prof. Gates were later dropped. It should be noted that when police officers receive a report that someone is possibly breaking into a house, and they arrive at that house and find somebody matching the description of the reported person, they have a duty to make sure that person actually belongs in the house.

President Barack Obama, during a nationally televised press conference to promote his health care plan told the nation that Prof. Gates was a friend of his, and said that he didn't know all the facts, but, "The Cambridge Police acted stupidly." That was very much less than helpful. I expected more from the President of the United States of America. A few days later, President Obama offered to host a gathering where the two men could get together and talk over a beer. Alcohol tends to cloud the mind and impair one's judgment. I think lunch would have been a better venue for the meeting, but then you probably couldn't set up the cameras far enough away to get pictures without being able to hear what was being said, in case all was not harmonious.

As a University Police Officer, I have been in many situations where someone tried to play the 'race card' or the 'status card'. Too many professors believe that they are above the laws and regulations that apply to all others. They are used to getting special treatment by the institution and demand special treatment at all times and in all situations.

The two 'cards' most often played in this country are the 'race card' and the 'status card'. An example of the 'status card' would be the executives who make decisions that nearly destroy a company financially, take a government bailout and then award themselves millions of dollars in bonuses, because they deserve them and are entitled to them. They think; no, they *know*, that they are better than the rest of us. Bernard Madoff could not have pulled off his massive Ponzi scheme if he did not believe he was above the law. These people, who, when stopped by the police for a traffic violation will demand special treatment. They will pull strings and try to have the officer fired, if the officer has the audacity to charge them with the violation. Bernard Madoff is serving a prison sentence of one hundred and fifty years, but I wonder how many months probation he would have been sentenced to serve, if he had swindled the common man instead of the very wealthy who also have 'status cards' themselves.

In my time living in New Orleans I saw many young blacks who appeared to be extremely angry. I have never seen people with so much anger. Then I met whites who were filled with hatred because of the color of someone's skin. They wanted to return to Segregation. These two groups seemed to be feeding off each other's hatred. I almost felt like I had traveled back in time to the 1950s. Thank God these two groups were in the minority. I often wondered how these two groups of people could live and work in the same geographic area and not kill each other, so great was their hatred for each other.

Hurricane Katrina did not care who she destroyed. Race or social status meant nothing to her. If either you; or your property were in her way, you lost. I saw whites, blacks, Asians, Native Americans and Latinos who lost everything. They lost property and many of them lost their lives. The wealthy as well as the poverty stricken also lost their lives. Who you were meant absolutely nothing to Katrina. Where you were at the time, determined whether she killed you or let you live. It was as simple as that.

When I was a police officer, I knew an officer from a neighboring department who used to say, "When my [butt] is getting kicked, I don't care what the color of the uniform coming through the door is." That would also apply to skin color. When you're getting thumped, all you want is some help. Racial, ethnic, or any other personal likes and dislikes go out the window. Two cops may have a great dislike, or even hatred for each other, but they are not going to let anything happen to the other one. They will put their differences aside if only for a little while. If only this would carry over into everyone's everyday life.

Lest someone think I'm naïve, I do know that there were some very disgusting and nasty incidents of racism in the wake of Katrina. I know what some of them were, and who committed them, including elected officials. However, I decided to write this book for healing purposes, and that would not be very healing. Because of that, and the fact that I did not see these incidents, I chose not to include them here. I am writing about what I saw and what I heard personally. I am very happy that I did not personally witness any racist incidents in the aftermath of Hurricane Katrina. I may write about them in some future work. Until that time, if I know you well enough, I may tell you about them in person.

As alive and well as racism was early in the twenty-first century in New Orleans, I never cease to be in amazement that after Katrina, I did not see anything racist. People did not care who they were helping; other people were in dire straits and they were willing to help. The victims sure as hell didn't care who was assisting them. They were in shock and despair and desperately in need of aid. What a great feeling to see everyone helping everyone. I am still in awe that all ethnic groups suffered and I personally saw people of all ethnic groups helping their brothers and sisters. No Color Barriers!

It is very sad that it took a major tragedy for people to put their differences aside, yet it's to their credit that they did. It's even sadder, however, that we have gone back to business as usual; hate someone because of the color of their skin, or the shape of their eyes or any other racial feature. We also use where a person's ancestors originated as a criteria to decide if we will like or hate them. What a foolish way to decide if we want to like someone.

When I'm talking with someone, I can tell you if they are white or black or Asian, etc. I can also tell you if they are tall or short, male or female, but that's as far as it goes. I am interested in the person, not the appearance. What do we have in common? What different interests do we have? How can we help to improve our lives, and the lives of our fellow man? These are the things that are truly important. It's time to stop playing the 'race card' and the 'status card'. When we do that we can live in harmony locally; then nationally. After that, perhaps we can learn to live together internationally. Wouldn't that be nice?

Race

Hurricanes don't care about the color of your face.
Katrina didn't care about status or national origin.
Humans are the only ones who can see color and race.
Color meant nothing as she wreaked havoc and ruin.

All ethnicities and races endured the same damage,
Whether a home, a relative or a friend didn't matter.
Major hurricanes make all classes and races scatter.
Katrina was an 'equal opportunity' cause of carnage.

Black, White, Asian, Native American and Latino,
All were Katrina's victims and suffered the same,
The helping hands I saw reaching out to all of us were
Black, White, Asian, Native American and Latino.

Recently, we had an ugly nationwide racial incident.
Someone decided to play the race card, and others,
Who probably needed the publicity added to the event
Making us look very foolish to many other nations.

During our recent disasters, Hurricane Katrina and 9-11,
We saw no color or race, only people in great need.
When will we ever learn that to be a great country indeed
Prejudice must go? Then we will truly be in heaven.

"I have a dream." Four famous words by Martin Luther King.
Equality and justice for all. All men living and working
Together in harmony. Remember our disasters.
There was no racism, just people aiding brothers and sisters.

Homes underwater in affluent neighborhood.
Photo courtesy of NOAA.

As the fourth anniversary of Hurricane Katrina approached, I was finishing this book. At first, I thought just publishing this work would be enough. Then I came to the realization that if I didn't write something for the fourth anniversary, I would be letting down those victims who can't speak for themselves.

"Four Years" is different from my other anniversary writings; it doesn't speak of rebuilding New Orleans or the Mississippi Gulf Coast. It speaks only of people; the victims and those who helped the victims of Hurricane Katrina.

I know many people curse Katrina because of what they lost; their injuries, and the loss of friends and relatives. This is a very normal reaction and I totally understand it. I have cursed many things and people who have caused me injury and pain.

The devastation from Hurricane Katrina was of monumental proportions. People lost everything whether they evacuated or not. Those who were fortunate enough not to be in the hurricane itself, still suffered. People were hurt physically, financially and emotionally. Some suffered all three types of injuries, even if they had fled the hurricane's path.

Man is a resilient animal. For the most part, he can recover from most injuries, both physical and psychological. There may be scars, but he usually heals. However, there are some injuries that are so severe, he can't recover. While I think of Katrina and her victims daily, as an anniversary approaches, I can't help but think about those victims who either perished at the time, or those poor suffering souls who will never be able to recover from Katrina's injuries. I feel their pain and wish I could make it go away. I can't, but I wish I could. If what I write can help in some small way, I have done my job. Maybe it can help a victim to know that others understand them. Maybe it will cause another person to do something to help them. The need for help will be there for many years.

As for me, I don't curse Hurricane Katrina. I am grateful God allowed me to experience Katrina because if I hadn't, I never would have changed. I would be the same negative person with a whole lot of anger. I would not be able to sit at my computer and share my thoughts with others. Yes, I did receive some loss, but compared to others, the harm I suffered was minor.

Now having said all that, I still think of Katrina as a Bitch!

Four Years

Katrina, four years have passed since you brought rain, and wind.
I think of you every day of my life. You have been cursed and
Damned for the suffering and pain, ruin and death you left behind.
It's amazing how you managed to change the lay of the land.

You broke men and women as you destroyed their lives.
You ruined homes, neighborhoods and whole communities,
Roads, buildings, even beaches, lakes, parks and gardens.
What you could never do is destroy the spirit of humans.

Some of my brothers and sisters will never recover
From the damage you did to them four years ago,
They will experience again your horror over and over.
Most however, will heal as on with their lives they go.

What you could never understand as you spread misery and pain,
As you left behind the dead and dying, miles of destruction,
People came from all over, their goal total resurrection,
To rebuild what you destroyed to its former glory once again.

Men and women, young, middle aged and older ones too,
All pitched in to help. Some in devastated areas assisting
With clean-up and rebuilding, others not handy with tools
Collecting food and clothing and getting them to victims.

I think of you every day. I remember what you did to a city
I love and its people. It didn't matter if they were poor or rich.
I remember you, but I don't curse you. I changed because of you.
No, Katrina, I don't curse you, but I still think of you as a Bitch!

It's been more than two and half years since Hurricane Katrina slammed into New Orleans and devastated the Mississippi Gulf Coast region. Until tonight (March 6, 2008) I have had no desire to try to describe that fateful night. All my poems and stories have been about what the storm did, what people did, and the effect the storm had on me. Tonight I have tried to show you Hurricane Katrina through my eyes and ears as witnessed from the 'relative safety' of the doorway of the Holiday Inn Express in downtown New Orleans, a block and a half from Bourbon Street and the French Quarter.

There is a hotel across the street from the Holiday Inn Express that closes whenever a hurricane is coming. When they closed for Hurricane Katrina, they threw their guests out. Two of those guests came in to the Holiday Inn Express to try to get a room. We were fully booked, but a couple who were leaving realized that these people were stranded. They said they had room in their car and would be happy to drive them to Alabama. I didn't realize it at the time, but I had just seen the first of Katrina's Angels in action.

When the hotel across the street closes for hurricanes, it allows New Orleans Police Officers to stay there while they are closed. Sunday night, August 28, 2005, a group of the police officers staying there were members of the SWAT Team of NOPD. They were partying heavily at the bar next door to our hotel. As a former police officer, I understand and have participated in the partying mentality. You know what you have just witnessed, or what you will be seeing in the near future. It's a release, not a healthy one, but a release. At any rate, these guys knew they would be seeing some very unpleasant things in the next few days. At that time, no one had any idea just how extensive the horror would be.

It was rather humorous watching them standing out in the street with water halfway up to their knees. This was before the hurricane actually hit. (Whenever there is heavy rain in New Orleans, the streets flood). As the winds picked up, they fought valiantly to stand there and brave the weather. Those guys were having fun, but they were smart enough to go inside before the wind became too strong. I'm sure they did not get to party again for a long time, as they were very busy for the next several weeks.

A couple of hours later, Hurricane Katrina began in earnest. As I stood there all night, I was in awe by the mighty power of the storm. Trees about two and a half inches in diameter were bent parallel to the sidewalk. The rain was completely horizontal and any object that blew by was completely unrecognizable as it went by at well over one hundred miles per hour. You just knew something went by, but there was no way to tell what it was. The roar of the wind can best be described as sounding like a jet engine out of control.

I remember being at a NASCAR race in Dover, DE and we wanted to get a 'quick start' leaving when the race was over. We stood at the fence at the bottom of the stands for the last few laps. That track is a one mile oval. It takes a little over twenty seconds to make a lap. That is a speed of over 150 miles per hour. As the cars went by, all you could see was a blur. You might pick out a color, but you couldn't make out the car. That is all I could think of when something blew by the hotel during Hurricane Katrina. I have often been asked if someone could have survived outside during Hurricane Katrina. The answer to that question is, "NO!" Unless you were sheltered, the wind would have blown away a grown man. Remember, Katrina was a Category 5 hurricane!

After the storm, flooding began as long-neglected levees were breached. Over eighty percent of the city wound up under water. Floodwaters contaminated with everything from dead bodies, fuel oil, garbage, raw sewage, fluids leaking out of every submerged vehicle, storage tanks giving up their contents to the floodwaters, all kinds of hazardous waste. God only knows what was in that water. For a couple of days, I waded through that water as I went about my duties. When I left the city, I had chemical burns on my legs. My doctor has told me that I will always get outbreaks of rashes on my legs as the skin was badly damaged. To this date, no one has said if there was anything in the water that will cause permanent problems. I have no medical degree, but two and a half years after Hurricane Karina, I still get outbreaks of rashes and itching not only on my legs, but also on my hands, upper arms and back, which were never under water. The water never got above my thighs. What was in the water that entered my body and never left? They said the air at Ground Zero was not dangerous, but five years later, people are dying from lung diseases caused by contaminants in the air at Ground Zero. Will we find down the road that Katrina's floodwaters will cause permanent damage to those who were in it?

The results of the storm have had a profound effect on many people, including me. It changed me forever in a positive way. I hope what I wrote will cause a change in you as well.

Storm

You came to town one day in late August,
A hazy, cloudy, warm and humid day.
Starting with a gentle rain and breeze,
Soon, torrential rain with powerful gusts.

A clamorous roar like a jet engine out of control,
All through the endless night you vented your fury.
Your rain came down sideways as your wind howled.
My ears ringing as I was fascinated by your potency.

Objects flying past my vantage point were unidentified
As they flew past at well over one hundred miles an hour
A part of a building, a car's hood or perhaps a street sign?
I watched in awe as this scene played on hour after hour.

After a long and terrifying night, you decided to move on.
Was your fury spent? Had you caused enough damage?
Had you finished killing? Could we now carry on as before?
Oh No! Your aftermath caused much more pain and carnage!

You breached levees and flooded eighty percent of the city.
You trapped people in attics while your filthy floodwaters
Swallowed entire houses; erased complete neighborhoods.
How many innocents did you kill as you ravaged the city?

Property damage measured in the many billions of dollars.
The human cost immeasurable in terms of cents and dollars.
You're still remembered long after you left the scene.
Who are you? You're that Bitch known as Katrina!

People who did not heed the warnings
were trapped in attics or on rooftops.
Photo courtesy of NOAA.

Epilogue

It's been nearly four years since Hurricane Katrina devastated New Orleans and the Mississippi Gulf Coast. Millions of lives were irrevocably changed in a matter of hours. I am one of those millions. However, my life was changed for the better. Unfortunately, many lives were destroyed. Many will never recover. During this time, I have been writing the stories and poems that make up "Memories of Hurricane Katrina and Other Musings".

Writing these stories and poems has been very healing for me. Expressing my feelings and thoughts on paper gave me the opportunity to pour out my emotions in the privacy of my own home. I could examine them, determine if they accurately represented what I felt, and make any corrections necessary. The best part was no one could see any of this until I was ready for them to do so. Now, I am ready to share these observations with the world. Some of my stories express anger, others hope, while still others show the goodness of man during a great tragedy.

I have heard a lot of criticism about the Federal Government's response to Hurricane Katrina. Having seen firsthand the incompetence and lack of preparation on the part of the local and state governments, I don't want to hear that criticism unless you were there. I will, however, defend your right to make your statements, and I will respect your beliefs. Please, just don't make those statements to me. After three days of hearing no news, only rumors, I can't tell you the sense of relief I felt hearing that President Bush was flying over New Orleans and that help was on the way. That was a hell of a lot more than the mayor or the governor was doing. Also, keep in mind that I knew that I would be leaving the city in about an hour. It didn't matter to me personally, but it would sure mean something to those wretched, suffering souls who could not leave.

Without going into any great detail, consider those two hundred school busses we all saw underwater in New Orleans. Loading fifty people on each of those busses would have taken ten thousand people out of the city and across Lake Pontchartrain. With a little planning and cooperation with St. Tammany Parish, those busses could have made several trips. St. Tammany parish could have brought those people to shelters further inland. (That's what is known as leadership; something not known to exist in the mayor's office or the governor's office at the time of Hurricane Katrina.) Instead, they were left behind to be flooded. You know a city the size of New Orleans has more than two hundred school busses. Firefighters from Peoria, Illinois were stuck in Baton Rouge because the state government refused to let them go to New Orleans to relieve their brother firefighters who were nearly exhausted.

Shortly after arriving in Massachusetts, I received a call on my cell phone. It was from a representative of MEMA, Massachusetts Emergency Management Agency. She told me that I should go to the Hynes Convention Center in Boston the following day as many relief agencies were going to be there to offer assistance to Katrina victims living in Massachusetts. Among the people I met there was a representative of FEMA, Federal Emergency Management Agency. The FEMA rep told me that she had been in Baton Rouge and that FEMA had been all set up and ready to go on Saturday August 27. She told me that the State of Louisiana made them move to another location. You don't set up an operation like that overnight. Thanks to the state, they were not ready when the storm struck. How many people died because of that kind of incompetence and inaction by the local and state governments?

My mind's eye reveals images of the New Orleans Superdome with its roof peeled back, like a giant orange, and I see thousands of people seeking refuge, and then in the middle of a monster hurricane, the building loses its roof. How terrified they must have been! Then I see them for the next several days trapped there with no food, no water, no power, no sanitary facilities and floodwaters rising all around them. Next, I see that elderly lady in her wheelchair outside the New Orleans Morial Convention Center. She had died and was left sitting in her wheelchair for days.

I see the looters, hear the gunfire and watch the buildings as they burn to the ground, the victims of arsonists. I see a sight I never thought I would see in the United States of America; I see a fuel oil truck with a New Orleans Police Officer on each running board holding a fully automatic M-16 assault rifle, and ready to use it against looters who might try to hijack the fuel oil truck. I see the destruction of a once magnificent city and tears come to my eyes.

One of the amazing things about the human mind is that it seeks to make one feel better. It doesn't dwell on the images I outlined above. It also shows vivid pictures of people reaching out to help other souls. I see people who have just lost everything trying to comfort a complete stranger. My mind's eye shows a wonderful woman who had lost everything she did not take with her when she left home before the storm, looking at me and saying, "I think you need a hug." Race did not matter. I see people of all races and colors helping other human beings. Katrina did not consider race in selecting her victims, and neither did those who gave a helping hand. I see a city, Houston, opening its arms and heart to complete strangers in an attempt to help their fellow man.

When I first left New Orleans, I was experiencing nightmares almost nightly. Now the nightmares are much less frequent. I'm sure they will always be there, but I can live with that. I had difficulty talking about my experience at first. It is much easier for me to speak about Hurricane Katrina; although there are a few things that I still won't talk about, and probably never will. That's also okay!

I have learned to deal with the effects of Katrina. One of the best things that happened to me was sitting in that hotel while the floodwater was rising and making peace with my Maker. My life changed that night; for the better! Examining my feelings also helped greatly. I could either write them down as a poem or story, or express them verbally to a friend. This allowed me to deal with the issues, rather than ignore them and try to suppress them. When the lights went out in New Orleans, I began to see. The darkness of the city truly opened my eyes and let me see. I have seen more deer in the past three years than I have ever seen in my entire life. They were always there; I just did not see them. I was too wrapped up in myself. Now I'll see a deer and thank God for that. I see the beauty in nature that I never saw before. I find it very soothing and calming. It also eases my mind and helps to replace unpleasant images. I can look at clouds and see shapes, as we all did as kids. How great is that?

In my years in New Orleans, either working as a House Detective for a hotel on Bourbon St. or as the Director of Security for another hotel chain, I had many dealings with the New Orleans Police Department, especially the officers of the Eighth District which covers the French Quarter and the Central Business District. I worked directly with many of them and they were very professional. I always received a prompt response from them.

119

Every month the Greater New Orleans Hotel/Motel Association held a meeting for the Directors of Security. The New Orleans Police Department Eighth District Commander and the officers were invited to attend. After that meeting, NOPD held its COMSTAT meeting, to which we were invited. There was a wonderful exchange of information, which was important to both the hotels and the police. It allowed us and the officers to get to know each other. In addition, it gave us the opportunity to coordinate activities between the police and the lodging industry to solve problems that affected us both.

We have heard some uncomplimentary reports about the actions of some New Orleans Police Officers in the wake of Katrina. Unfortunately, I saw some of that conduct by a few officers. Police officers are people and have the same shortcomings other people have. However, most of the officers I knew or saw in New Orleans, including during and after Hurricane Karina were hard working men and women doing a difficult, thankless job. I have to point out as an example, the officer who was in his sixties, who lived in his cruiser for several months. He did his job every day, and since he lost his house, slept in his cruiser and cleaned up in a WalMart washroom.

I had many dealings with the police dispatchers, although nothing on a face to face basis. These women were all very professional, although some were more personable than others. All did an outstanding job in any of the dealings I had with them. They not only listened to the caller; they also listened to the background noises and prioritized their response accordingly. I mention them because they went through their own particular hell during and immediately after Katrina struck. I don't know how any of them survived without extensive counseling. They are certainly in my thoughts and prayers along with the other Katrina victims.

Someday someone is going to use the Freedom of Information Act to get the 911apes from Hurricane Katrina. I hope this never happens, but if it does, please heed this advice, DO NOT listen to them or read their transcripts! If you do, you will never sleep again! I know what's on a couple of those tapes and I wish to God that I didn't.

What I did not mention in this work were the victims of Hurricane Rita. Less than a month after Katrina, Hurricane Rita struck Louisiana west of New Orleans as well as southeast Texas. Those kind people who had escaped Katrina, but were so willing to help Katrina's victims, became victims themselves. I didn't write about Rita's victims and experiences because I did not go through Rita. I do, however, relate to you on two levels, the first is we both survived hurricanes and more importantly, is the fact that you were there to assist me and other Katrina victims, less than a month before you became victims yourselves.

There is a special empathy in my heart and prayers for Katrina's victims, for Rita's victims and for the victims of all natural disasters. You cannot go through one of these without developing a special affinity for others who have also experienced one of these tragedies.

A Final Word

I had just about finished this manuscript when something amazing happened; but first a little background. I have had a difficult time every August since Katrina. Look at my anniversary poems and stories and you will see that. This year, 2009 was no exception. One day about a week ago, a friend came up to me at breakfast and asked how I was doing. I knew by the way she had asked that that she had sensed how I was feeling; not real great! I replied that I was okay and let it go at that. The following Saturday, August 15, 2009, I was driving by her house and saw her doing yard work. I honked the horn and waved as I drove by. Then I did something very unusual for me. I turned around and went back to her house. She was finishing her yard work for the day so I helped her put the tools away. She invited me in for a cold drink.

I asked her if she had picked up something in me earlier in the week. She said that she had noticed something wasn't right. I told her about August being a tough month for me. She said that I should not be down for an entire month. I then did something very rare for me. I opened up about my experiences with Katrina and its aftermath. When I arrived in Massachusetts in 2005, I had a few sessions with a professional counselor. Other than that, the only person I had really confided in was Cailin Reiken, a close friend, who happens to be a mental health counselor, during our massage sessions. Dr. Frances Rahaim has a PhD in finance. It seems that synchronicity played a big role last Saturday. Frances made a couple of suggestions and let me borrow a book that she thought might be helpful. The book, "The Secret" by Rhonda Byrne has been very inspirational to me. I saw Cailin the following Monday and told her about how much better I had been feeling since Saturday. I told her about "The Secret" and she said that until now that book probably would not have helped because I was not ready for it. Now that I am ready, it is very helpful. Synchronicity: events seemingly coincidental, coming together in a certain time and place. Why did I drive that route to where I was going? There were three other ways I could have gone. Why did I stop at my friend's house on Saturday? Why did I decide to open up at that time? All I know is I have felt better since Saturday.

Now the amazing thing I told you about. While going through this manuscript and retyping and editing it, I made an amazing discovery. Much of my writing, especially around each anniversary had to do with my concern for the victims. They are foremost in my mind. I suddenly realized that I was feeling guilt. Was that survivor's guilt still hanging around? I thought that I had gotten rid of that. What I realized is that for twenty-one years I had been a police officer. I had always gone to help victims when something happened. After Katrina, I left town! Once I realized what was bugging me, I was able to see that I was not in a position to rescue people back then. I had done my job in doing my part to keep the people in the hotel safe and getting them evacuated. I would only have been in the way and perhaps put myself in a position where I would need to be rescued. I finally realized that I had made the best decision for everybody four years ago.

I don't have that depression nagging at me anymore. I know that on the twenty-ninth of August, I'll hold my own memorial service; remember Katrina, pray for the victims. Then I'll move on. It took me four years, but now I'm letting you go. Goodbye, Katrina!